KENDALL FEAVER received a Judges Award at the 2015 Bruntwood Prize for Playwriting, Best New Play at the 2018 UK Theatre Awards, the 2019 Victorian Premier's Prize Drama, and the 2019 Nick Enright Prize for Playwriting for her play *The Almighty Sometimes* (Royal Exchange, Manchester; Griffin Theatre Company, Sydney). She has written on attachment at the National Theatre Studio and the Bush Theatre, was the 2019 Philip Parsons Fellow at Belvoir Street Theatre, and a Genesis Almeida Writer (2019/20). Her play *Wherever She Wanders* (Griffin Theatre Company 2021) was highly commended for the 2020 Victorian Premier's Prize. Kendall is currently developing new plays and musicals with the National Theatre, Almeida Theatre, Manhattan Theatre Club, and Belvoir; and a film for Pathé UK.

*Tom Conroy and Nikki Shiels in Belvoir's 2021 production of* My Brilliant Career. *(Photo: BrettBoardman)*

THE PLAY

by **KENDALL FEAVER**

Based on the novel by Miles Franklin

**CURRENCY PRESS**
The performing arts publisher

CURRENCY PLAYS

First published in 2021
by Currency Press Pty Ltd,
PO Box 2287, Strawberry Hills, NSW, 2012, Australia
enquiries@currency.com.au
www.currency.com.au



Typeset by Dean Nottle for Currency Press.
Printed by Fineline Print + Copy Services, Revesby, NSW.
Cover design by Emma Bennetts for Currency Press.
Cover features Nikki Shiels, photo by Daniel Boud.

A catalogue record for this book is available from the National Library of Australia

# Contents

*From left: Jason Chong, Nikki Shiels, Tom Conroy and Emma Harvie in Belvoir's 2021 production of* My Brilliant Career. *(Photo: BrettBoardman)*

# INTRODUCTION

AUNT HELEN: Sybylla, I wonder—…? Does every thought of yours need to be articulated?
SYBYLLA: But—… I have so many—?

Sybylla Melvyn and Kendall Feaver have something in common: so many ideas.

To read or see a Kendall Feaver play is to witness an idea at its ignition point, following its journey as it grows, tests its limits, and finds a place to land.

And Sybylla Melvyn knows a thing or two about testing limits. The central protagonist in the 1901 novel *My Brilliant Career* and now this play, she is a teenager from a rural New South Wales on the brink of Australia's Federation. Sybylla has a wild hunger for life: she wants to be an artist, a musician, a traveller, a writer. Never a wife, though, and never a mother.

But of course, wifedom and motherhood is the path expected for women at the time, especially women who, like Sybylla, are not wealthy. Sybylla, however, is alight with thought: she knows she must be louder beyond the point of politeness to be heard. And so she just keeps on talking.

Feaver and Sybylla's creator, Stella Maria Sarah Miles Franklin, have a driving hunger in common—their writing is a restless, living thing. Feaver prowls around problems until she understands them, and Franklin, through the voice of Sybylla, barrels through them—fighting it all the while. But Franklin and Feaver ultimately both arrive in the same place: in the very centre of a feeling.

Then they offer it up to us, both the beauty and ugliness, so we can feel it too. Centuries apart, they are telling the same story of what it means to have something to say in a world that doesn't want to hear it.

Each is a force of nature. Together, they are dazzling.

*My Brilliant Career, The Play* is a direct address, a love letter, a tumult, a portrait. It is brimming with urgency—Sybylla's, yes, but Feaver's too—to be understood.

The beauty of this adaptation is that, in Feaver's hand, it ensures we understand each and every moment.

Sybylla Melvyn looms large in Australian culture and bears more than a passing resemblance to a young Franklin. A member of the colonising squattocracy, she submitted her manuscript to writer and poet Henry Lawson, who sent it on to his publisher in Edinburgh. At that stage, the novel was called *My Brilliant (?) Career* and she had chosen the pen name Miles Franklin to conceal her gender; she'd started submitting pieces to the *Daily Telegraph* and the *Sydney Morning Herald* at the same time, using pseudonyms such as 'An Old Bachelor'.

But *My Brilliant Career*, as a work, is dotted with little betrayals. Lawson refused to conceal Franklin's identity, outing her as a 'a little bush girl' in the book's introduction. Franklin wrote about people and places she knew, sometimes unflatteringly so; the outcry from those who knew her eventually resulted in her pulling the book from publication until after her death. And, famously, her title was altered without her consent—a question mark removed from the middle of the phrase, denying Franklin the twist of irony she intended.

Two major literary prizes are named for Franklin, who is simultaneously a ballast for women who write new Australias with their stories and also a symbol of a nation still stymied by its fondness for particular narratives: pastoral, white, settler-focused, male-centred.

But as a symbol, Sybylla Melvyn endures.

Now, Kendall Feaver has brought *My Brilliant Career* to the Australian stage. It's as though we've always been waiting for her there.

But perhaps Sybylla was waiting for Kendall Feaver.

> SYBYLLA: Why did you make me this way? Why fill me with cruel ambition and then set me down in a time and place where I can do nothing about it?

Here, Feaver takes a work with a long history and not a little notoriety—and then lifts it out of the now-tired hands of its first showing. She makes it something bigger, something more present—in conversation with all of us in the here and now, more than a hundred years on, who are still fighting for rights, recognition and respect.

This adaptation is a patchwork-puzzle of invention that draws dashes of text and generous spirit from the novel, its sequel *My Career Goes Bung* and beyond into Franklin's other writing. The final product is a closely guided study of a restless, Romantic heart.

Feaver anchors her whole play around Sybylla's narration. This script is thrumming and busy, but not over-burdened; the matter of living is brisk and no-nonsense here, and while Sybylla directly addresses the audience to claim the time as her own and re-frame it through her own perspective, it does not slow down for her. It does not wait to be made into art. She is not in control not of the events, but of the telling, which allows for flashes of brilliance—where imagination and perception collide with reality. This script has a lot of room for play. It thrives in the space between exaggeration and brutal honesty.

Feaver takes great care to demonstrate Sybylla's adolescent overreactions, but she places even more care on communicating when her anger is righteous.

> SYBYLLA: That was my first kiss.
>
> *Beat.*
>
> That was my first ever kiss and you took it from me.

Through the story, Sybylla is touched without her consent by any manner of men. In Franklin's original text, it could not quite yet be articulated that Sybylla's body was truly her own; the casually predatory behaviour and laughingly inflicted sexual slights.of the time were a burden to be endured.

Here, Feaver places them in their true and devastating context—as harassment and thoughtless assault—and in so doing, she serves to anchor Sybylla's too-loud self-assertions in an entirely reasonable motivation: to honour her selfhood. No-one will let Sybylla claim her own worth; Feaver shows us how she must take it for herself.

Like the book, Feaver's Sybylla dreams of being an artist. She wants to matter; she wants to leave her mark on the world. With Feaver's sparkling wit and sensitivity, the story builds: after a brief hint of hope in the home of her wealthier grandmother, her family's circumstances return to constrain her: she is sent to work as a governess for a large family.

The losses land fast and furious, a carefully placed act-break elevating the point of despair. No more those plans to go to Sydney and make something of herself. Gone, too, is a romance that near-turned Sybylla's head (though she will insist her story is not a love story). Like her mother before her, Sybylla is relegated to serving others. She tries to subdue her dreams.

But Sybylla keeps on living.

Feaver's play finds every moment it can to give every woman in the story a voice, feelings, and purpose. Each one—from the rough-edged Mrs McSwat to refined Grannie, is given pleasing grit. The men around Sybylla—her alcoholic father, her dilletante uncle, her fair-weather love interest Harry Beecham—are great characters, bearing many of the laugh lines and allowing for pathos. However, while they bring Sybylla shallow pleasures, they much more frequently bring her disappointment.

It's the quiet solidarity of women—in a variety of forms—that helps build Sybylla's bluster in more sustainable strength. Living with Grannie expands Sybylla's world view and helps her to better understand herself; her Aunt Helen offers advice; Beecham's spinster aunt Gussie shows the steel of women who survive alone.

She begins to carry these women with her; when Sybylla becomes a worker, the weary lines spoken at the beginning of the play by Mary O'Farrell, her grandmother's maid, find a new home in Sybylla's mouth. She understands her better now.

Feaver also brings this sense of perspective, and of respect, to the character of Lucy, Sybylla's mother. Through her curious, compassionate playwright's gaze, Feaver understands that while Lucy can't quite speak her fondness for her daughter, she loves her ferociously. Her love is all action without words, but when the time does come to speak it, Feaver ensures we see that Lucy's harshness with Sybylla is a tool of living, one she wants her daughter to learn:

> LUCY: You seem to live in a dream world, Sybylla, where the undeniable fact of your sex will be ignored—nay—celebrated! But I live in this one. And if my daughter cannot thrive in it, I want her to at least survive it.

This play takes an old Australian story and pushes it into the future with a modern sensibility and a genuine sense of care. Sybylla is our beacon, our lens through which we focus on the enduring human struggle to be seen, heard, and understood.

Beyond the page and stage, there is more work to do to ensure that every Australian can speak their mind and be their true selves, without fear. But for now, in the timeless pages of this play, Sybylla's unflinching devotion to her true self may encourage others to develop a better relationship to their own hopes, dreams, and inner life. She just might compel you to raise your voice and speak out.

*Cassie Tongue*
*Sydney, October 2021*

Cassie Tongue is a theatre critic and arts/culture writer living in Sydney on unceded Gadigal land. She writes for a variety of publications including: the *Sydney Morning Herald*, *Guardian Australia*, *Saturday Paper* and ABC online.

*For Vinay Patel*

## AUTHOR'S NOTE

Sybylla Penelope Melvyn has a complicated relationship with most things.

She has no desire to be a man but rails against the act of biological sabotage that is sometimes being a woman. She sneers at romance and simultaneously describes herself as a creature *hungry* for love. And in the end, she writes, not necessarily because she's found her artistic destiny (as we might expect from a story of this kind) but from a distinct lack of other options. More so, I suspect, she writes from a defiant need to 'voice' herself into existence.

And what a voice! Angry and strident. Playful and provocative. Strikingly postmodern in parts. Despite the century between us, I feel deep affinity to this one-hundred-and-twenty-years-old teenager. All those long run-on sentences! The prolific use of exclamation marks and CAPITAL LETTERS! And of course … her stubborn desire to live life on her own terms, and at any cost.

But the history of *My Brilliant Career* is itself complicated. Henry Lawson and the Scottish editors famously ignored a young Stella Franklin's request to be known as a male author (they kept her middle-name-pseudonym 'Miles' but outed her as 'just a little bush girl' in the preface). They also removed the ironic question mark from the title—*My Brilliant (?) Career*—and cut what they deemed to be the more 'salacious' paragraphs. (What were these? As the original proofs don't exist—we don't know!) And despite the critical and commercial success of her book, Franklin later withdrew it from publication, struggling with accusations that her fiction was more biographical than not, and overwhelmed too at seeing her intimate and very teenage thoughts printed and for posterity. Almost immediately, she wrote another book—a satirical corrective—*My Career Goes Bung*—which Australian publishers felt was too audacious to print. It wasn't published for another 40 years.

So, how to approach an adaptation of a book that shifts and moves, depending on the lens through which you're looking? As Franklin herself later admitted that *My Brilliant Career* was thinly-veiled autobiography, I felt comfortable casting the net wider than the original book, drawing from *My Career Goes Bung*, her childhood memoirs, and the work of her biographers, all to gain some deeper sense of this Stella/Miles/Sybylla hybrid. Of particular interest was her relationship with her mother, Susannah Lampe Franklin, a woman who dragged a piano across a mountain range, spent the first thirteen years of marriage almost consistently pregnant, and lived to see all but two children pass away. This was also a woman who (possibly) burned her daughter's writing in the stove, yet, in later years, carefully preserved the only copy of *My Career Goes Bung*—in such contradictions, great characters are made!

Within this adaptation, some words remain Franklin's, some words are my own, but where it was necessary to depart from the original novel, I have tried to be faithful in capturing language, tone and energy. The goal of this script, ultimately, was to create an architecture that would allow for play, problem-solving and endless creativity in production. I hope this is exactly what it inspires. And while this is a version of *My Brilliant Career* that does lean towards youthful exuberance, righteous anger and the thrill of first love, there are still jagged edges in here, moments that sting and wound. It was a revelation to discover, for example, that Franklin's much-loved little sister Linda married a man who had previously proposed to Franklin. But Linda never recovered from the birth of her first child. She died several months later and not before writing to Franklin of some of the horrors of her wedding night—'I really wished I would die'. For all of Franklin's witty posturing on marriage as 'the most horribly tied-down and unfair-to-women existence going', the threat of it—to her identity, to her autonomy, to her economic security, to her ambitions, to her physical wellbeing—was very real.

In some ways, Franklin was astonishingly ahead of her time, constructing a feminism that would not be out of place with young women at a public protest today. But it needs to be acknowledged that Franklin's is an incomplete feminism with limited understanding of First Nations or other settler populations. Likewise, her portrayals of Australia are, occasionally, myopic—fuelled by a nostalgia for a time and place that existed in the imaginations of bush poets, but less so in reality.

Still, to badly paraphrase her contemporary, Virginia Woolf: the fact that a woman, from this time, wrote anything at all, can be considered an enormous achievement. I think we can celebrate Franklin in her tenacity, while acknowledging that the barriers she faced also speak to the enormous wastage of so many other people—both men and women—trapped in circumstances beyond their control. To the extent that this is a period piece, there's something profound, also, in considering how much has changed since 1899, and how much hasn't changed at all.

My heartfelt thanks to Louise Gough and Eamon Flack, whose dramaturgy on this has been exceptional. To the original cast and creatives for their insightful notes, particularly Nikki Shiels, the hardest working actress I know. To Hannah Goodwin, who kept me (mostly) sane in 'what was a difficult year', and of course, to the play's director, Kate Champion. As a young(ish) writer of the female persuasion, I am very aware that my pathway to 'a career' was forged by so many women before me. The importance of seeing an artistic lineage cannot be underestimated. It is an honour to revisit Miles Franklin's 1901 text, to build on the 1979 film legacy created by Gillian Armstrong, Margaret Fink and Eleanor Whitcombe; and to work, in the here and now, with Kate Champion and her brilliant team.

I am so proud to be a part of this.

*Kendall Feaver*
*December 2020*

As a tiny child I was filled with dreams of the great things I was to do … As I grew it dawned on me that I was a girl—the makings of a woman! … It came home to me a great blow that it was only men who could take the world by its ears and conquer their fate, while women, metaphorically speaking, were forced to sit with tied hands and patiently suffer as the waves of fate tossed them hither and thither, battering and bruising without mercy …

'… Action! Action! Give me action!' was my cry.

Sybylla Melvyn
*My Brilliant Career*

*My Brilliant Career* was first produced at Belvoir Theatre, Sydney, on 5 December 2021 with the following cast:

| | |
|---|---|
| LUCY BOSSIER MELVYN / AUNT HELEN / MRS MCSWAT | Blazey Best |
| RICHARD MELVYN / UNCLE JAY JAY / MR MCSWAT | Jason Chong |
| HORACE MELVYN / FRANK HAWDEN / PETER MCSWAT JNR | Tom Conroy |
| GERTIE MELVYN / MARY O'FARRELL / BLANCHE DERRICK / LIZER MCSWAT | Emma Harvie |
| GRANDMA BOSSIER / AUNT GUSSIE / MIDWIFE / KATIE MCSWAT | Tracy Mann |
| SYBYLLA PENELOPE MELVYN | Nikki Shiels |
| HAROLD BEECHAM / TRAMP / TOMMY MCSWAT / JIMMY MCSWAT / ROSE-JANE MCSWAT | Guy Simon |

Director, Kate Champion
Set and Costume Designer, Robert Cousins
Lighting Designer, Amelia Lever-Davidson
Composer, Chrysoulla Markoulli
Sound Designer, Steve Francis
Fight and Movement Director, Nigel Poulton
Assistant Director, Hannah Goodwin
Dialect Coach, Jennifer White
Stage Manager, Luke McGettigan
Assistant Stage Manager, Ayah Tayeh

## CHARACTERS

SYBYLLA PENELOPE MELVYN
RICHARD MELVYN
LUCY BOSSIER MELVYN
GERTIE MELVYN
HORACE MELVYN
MIDWIFE
GRANDMA 'GRANNIE' BOSSIER
AUNT HELEN BELL
UNCLE JULIUS JOHN 'JAY JAY' BOSSIER
FRANK HAWDEN
MARY O'FARRELL
TRAMP/S
HAROLD 'HARRY' BEECHAM
AUNT AUGUSTA 'GUSSIE' BEECHAM
BLANCHE DERRICK
MR MCSWAT
MRS MCSWAT
PETER MCSWAT JNR
LIZER MCSWAT
JIMMY MCSWAT
TOMMY MCSWAT
ROSE-JANE MCSWAT
KATIE MCSWAT
CHILDREN

Recommended Doubling:

SYBYLLA PENELOPE MELVYN
LUCY BOSSIER MELVYN / AUNT HELEN / MRS MCSWAT
RICHARD MELVYN / UNCLE JAY JAY / MR MCSWAT
GERTIE MELVYN / MARY O'FARRELL / BLANCHE DERRICK / LIZER MCSWAT
HORACE MELVYN / FRANK HAWDEN / PETER MCSWAT JNR
GRANDMA BOSSIER / AUNT GUSSIE / MIDWIFE / KATIE MCSWAT
HAROLD BEECHAM / TRAMP / TOMMY MCSWAT / JIMMY MCSWAT / ROSE-JANE MCSWAT

## SETTING

Rural New South Wales, 1890 to 1899, verdant mountain gullies through to drought-stricken plains.

## NOTES

This script was originally written for an ensemble of seven actors and with the intention that contemporary modes of theatre making—music, movement, physical inventiveness (etc)—play some significant part. To that end, there are many rapid changes in character and location. Speed, mostly, and fluidity, always, is key.

**Bold type** indicates Sybylla's direct address to the audience.

*The playwright asks that casting, for all future productions, continues to reflect the diversity of modern-day Australia.*

*From left: Guy Simon, Emma Harvie, Nikki Shiels and Tracy Mann in Belvoir's 2021 production of* My Brilliant Career. *(Photo: BrettBoardman)*

# ACT ONE

## *ONE: AN INTRODUCTION*

SYBYLLA. *Aged nineteen.*

*She speaks from the end and simultaneously the beginning.*

SYBYLLA: **This story is all about myself.**

**For this, I make no apologies.**

**Other autobiographies weary one with their excuses for egotism.**

**If I am egotistical, what matters it to you?**

**You don't know me from a basket of gooseberries, and won't if I only keep myself to myself, and as I can't—here I am!—and I will endure the embarrassment of bringing myself to your attention again—**

MIDWIFE: [*faintly*] Sybylla—

SYBYLLA: **And again—**

MIDWIFE: [*louder*] *Sybylla—*

SYBYLLA: **And again and again and again and again—!**

*The scene bursts into focus:* LUCY, *dripping in sweat, braces herself against the kitchen table. A local* MIDWIFE *bustles about.* SYBYLLA, *now ten years old, and little sister* GERTIE, *do their best to help. If men are present, they wait outside ...*

MIDWIFE: Now now, Mrs Melvyn, I don't like interfering with what the good Lord has determined, but the good Lord, in all his wisdom, decided Mrs Ellis, two towns over, should find herself this same day confined, so you and I ... we might need to hurry this along juuust a little ...

*The* MIDWIFE *reaches her hand between* LUCY*'s legs in an attempt to break her waters.* LUCY *gasps with the new sensation and pain.*

SYBYLLA: **This is not a romance.**

MIDWIFE: Weeell done, Mrs Melvyn, well done.

SYBYLLA: **This is *not* a romance.**

MIDWIFE: Sybylla, take this pot—fill it with water—Gertie dear, come and take these rags, that's a good girl—

SYBYLLA: **Do not fear encountering such TRASH as descriptions of sunsets, tall trees in silhouette or whisperings of wind—HA! I am too often starved of hours in my day to waste time snivelling and gushing over fancies and dreams—**

MIDWIFE: Sybylla—?

SYBYLLA: **Neither is this a novel or—or a poem—!**

MIDWIFE: Sybylla—?

SYBYLLA: **—but something real—**

MIDWIFE: *Where* is that water—?!

SYBYLLA: **—*really* real—**

MIDWIFE: Sybylla—!

SYBYLLA: **—as real as weariness and—and bitter heartache! As real as the tall gum trees among which I first saw the light! As real as—!**

MIDWIFE: There you are! [*Taking the water*] Useless lump of a girl! Eldest daughter and can't help your poor mother? Out! Out from under my feet—!

SYBYLLA *and* GERTIE *both try to leave.*

—Nooo—I'll need at least one of you—so who's it going to be then?

*Beat.*

SYBYLLA: I'll set the table every day for six weeks—

GERTIE: No you won't—

SYBYLLA: Three weeks—

GERTIE: One—

SYBYLLA: Done.

SYBYLLA *kisses her sister on the cheek then makes a break for it.*

MIDWIFE: Alright, Mrs Melvyn, if you feel like pushing— …?

SYBYLLA: **As real as LIFE—!**

*From* LUCY, *a deep guttural groan, which may or may not take us through to the next scene ...*

**—provided life is anything other than heartless illusion, then here it is ... and here is where it begins!**

*TWO: I REMEMBER, I REMEMBER*

*An imaginary shoot-out is taking place between ten-year-old* SYBYLLA *and a couple of local boys.*

SYBYLLA: **Ten years old, and at that tender stage in chrysalis where little boys dream of becoming engine drivers or champion boxers.**

*She downs a little boy.*

**Nothing so garishly simple for me.**

LUCY, *with the new baby.*

LUCY: Sybylla! I didn't mend that skirt so it could be trussed up around your waist!

SYBYLLA: You can't be a bushranger in a skirt, Mother.

LUCY: So come inside and I'll find you something more suitable to occupy your time with.

RICHARD: Leave her alone, Lucy.

LUCY: Your daughter is running around the front lawn in her undergarments—

RICHARD: She's a child—

LUCY: She's a young woman—

RICHARD: Which'll catch up with her soon enough. You let her be.

SYBYLLA: **My father has no patience for fairytales. Instead we read the biographies of GREAT people to learn how they conducted their business. Seeing the multitude of men in these pages, I ask**—There have been great women, haven't there, Pa?

RICHARD: There have been, and are, and will be yet.

SYBYLLA: Then I will be one of them!

*She shoots at another of the little boys.*

I got you, Podgy! Don't you dare move when you should be dead! DIE, PODGY! DIE DIE DIE—!

LUCY: [*to* RICHARD] You can't be anything without means.

RICHARD: A little common sense and a lot of passion, that's all you need.

LUCY: If that's all you need, then you and I should be living like kings.

RICHARD: A man can't make his fortune working his wife's estate.

LUCY: It's served you well enough so far—

RICHARD: [*trying to embrace her*] Ah, but maybe I desire more— …

LUCY: *Sybylla—!*

SYBYLLA: Catch me—Pa—!

*She launches herself at* RICHARD.

**… I learn how to float on my back in the clear mountain rivers …**

**… to dispatch a snake with a stock-whip …**

**… to ride horses with the best of them—side-saddle, man-saddle, no-saddle, and standing up like a circus queen—!**

*Her younger siblings,* HORACE *and* GERTIE, *enter and race around them.* HORACE *is plaguing* GERTIE *with a slug on a stick.*

GERTIE: / Syb! Syb! Syyyyyyyyb!

HORACE: Touch the slug, Gertie! Go on, scaredy—touch the slug!

SYBYLLA *leaps down to* GERTIE*'s rescue, while* LUCY, *mid-argument, grasps a land permit.*

LUCY: Possum Gully?! A hundred acres isn't enough to run cattle, Richard, it's barely enough for a dairy! What do you mean in buying this?!

SYBYLLA: [*still tussling with her siblings*] What did you buy, Pa?

RICHARD: [*intervening*] A new home, Sybbie, with the most thrilling sight in existence!

CHILDREN: What?

RICHARD: A road!

CHILDREN: [*deeply unimpressed*] A road?

RICHARD: Direct from the front paddock to the city of Goulburn, which has a train station that leads to Sydney—

CHILDREN: Sydney!

RICHARD: —and from there a sea track that meets the world!

LUCY: But what kind of business are you planning to run?

RICHARD: I'll deal in stock. Become an auctioneer, perhaps. Any number of things—

LUCY: But which one—?

RICHARD: Don't worry, my love. It's just a bit of land to get along with—

LUCY: / Until—?

RICHARD: —until we have the means to purchase more.

SYBYLLA: **My father has an answer for everything—!**

RICHARD: [*scooping her up, or some such*] Say goodbye to Caddagat, Sybbie!

SYBYLLA: Goodbye, Caddagat, goodbye!

RICHARD: Gertie? Horace?

GERTIE: Goodbye, Caddagat! HORACE: Goodbye!

RICHARD: You too, Lucy.

LUCY *remains silent. Stares at the only home she's ever known.*

SYBYLLA: **Behind me, I leave my childhood glinting on fern-banked streams. Ahead—a blue OCEAN of adventure calling with a deafening invitation to embark—!**

LUCY: Sybylla! Down from there!

SYBYLLA *clambers down.*

All play, no work or worry … you'll find life a different matter.

SYBYLLA: **LIFE a different matter!**

**I should *hope* so—!**

*THREE: POSSUM GULLY*

SYBYLLA. *Aged fifteen.*

SYBYLLA, GERTIE, HORACE *and* RICHARD *are trying to pull up an emaciated cow.*

RICHARD: Alright … *pull!*

*Pull!*

*Pull!* Get up, you great ugly beast—

SYBYLLA: Pa—wait—

RICHARD: Get up! Get up, I said!

HORACE: Pa—

RICHARD: Get up!

*Losing patience,* RICHARD *begins beating the cow.*

SYBYLLA: Pa—no! *No!* Stop it! Pa—!

RICHARD: If the cow stays down, it dies—

SYBYLLA: Stop it—*please*—!

RICHARD: Stupid, *stupid* animal—

SYBYLLA: She's tired—she's hungry—you can't expect her to—!

*A shocking crack as* RICHARD *shoots the cow.*

*No sound now except* GERTIE*'s deep intake of breath.*

RICHARD: You lot get back to the house. I'll go ask Mr Grady to help with this.

*He turns to leave.*

SYBYLLA: Are you going straight there, / Pa?

HORACE: [*warning*] Syb.

*Beat.*

RICHARD: I don't see how that's any concern of yours, Sybylla—?

SYBYLLA: If you end up at the pub, I'm the one who has to collect you—

RICHARD: DON'T you talk to me like that.

*Beat.*

If you have something to say, you bloody well keep it to yourself.

RICHARD *exits.*

SYBYLLA*, shaking with rage, grabs a knife and sharpens it.*

HORACE: Well done, Syb. If he wasn't heading there already, he sure as hell is now.

SYBYLLA: Ma cleared him out this morning. He thinks he's got shillings in his pocket; he hasn't got more than a couple of pennies.

HORACE: You shouldn't go on at him like that—

SYBYLLA: He's disgusting—

HORACE: Riling him up, making it harder for everyone else—

GERTIE: [*still staring at the cow*] Was she mine?

*Beat.*

Or yours?

*Beat.*

I can't— … I can't really tell anymore …?

SYBYLLA: Mine.

GERTIE *sighs with relief.*

GERTIE: It's not Pa's fault, you know. He can't help there's a drought.

HORACE: The Gradys and the O'Briens have a drought too: they make more butter than us—

GERTIE: The Gradys lost six cows last week—

SYBYLLA: But not from wanton assault! What's the point, Gertie?! What's the point in caring for them, day after day after day, if he's just going to—if he's just—?!

SYBYLLA *wants to cry but braces herself instead to remove the cow's hide.*

LUCY *appears, carrying a baby.*

*She turns at the sight of the cow.*

LUCY: That's enough.

GERTIE *and* HORACE *step away.* SYBYLLA *doesn't even look up.*

Sybylla, I said that's enough—

SYBYLLA: The hide needs to come off if we're to have anything to sell—

LUCY: We'll get one of the neighbours to do it—

SYBYLLA: With what money shall we pay them—?

LUCY: Sybylla, you've never cut the hide off a cow in your life, and I won't have you doing it now out of spite.

SYBYLLA *throws down the knife and moves quickly towards the house.*

Sybylla!

*Sybylla!*

## *FOUR: A LIVING*

SYBYLLA *races inside, rips off her dirty pinafore, and plunges her hands into a washbasin. She scrubs herself, still reeling with rage. Hearing* LUCY *approach,* SYBYLLA *lunges for the piano. She plays some simple jovial refrain, albeit badly.*

LUCY *enters, breathless, puts the baby down in its cradle.*

LUCY: Sybylla— …

SYBYLLA *cuts her off with the piano.*

Sybylla— …

*And again.*

Sybylla, please—

SYBYLLA: Why do we have a piano if we're not allowed to play it—?

LUCY: You're allowed to play it / when the chores are— …

SYBYLLA: When the chores are done, when the children are in bed, when father isn't *drunk*—

LUCY: You don't think I'd like to play it sometime—?

SYBYLLA: So why don't you?

LUCY: Because there are always more important things to do, no matter how dull they may seem to you—

SYBYLLA: Why not turn it around, Mother? Drive out dullness with the piano—!

LUCY *closes the lid, almost catching* SYBYLLA*'s fingers.*

*Silence.*

LUCY: Sybylla, I need to talk to you.

SYBYLLA: **What will it be tonight?**

LUCY: I've been studying the matter a lot lately—

SYBYLLA: **My capacity to oversleep? My unintentional breakage of a common cup? The need to honour thy parents whether they are deserving of it or *not*—**

LUCY: We can't afford to keep you here any longer.

SYBYLLA *turns to her mother. This is unexpected.*

We shall have to find some way for you to make a living.

SYBYLLA: A living?

LUCY: Yes.

SYBYLLA: As what?

LUCY: Well … you haven't taken to sewing. You don't have enough schooling to be a teacher. There's no chance in you being accepted as a hospital nurse, / so—

SYBYLLA: So I suppose it's a life of music then?

*Beat.*

LUCY: Music—?

SYBYLLA: I'll be a pianist. I'll play with the symphony orchestra—!

LUCY: You're not good enough—

SYBYLLA: I'll take lessons.

LUCY: With what time? What money?

SYBYLLA: I could be Mozart, Mother—

LUCY: What are you babbling on about now—?

SYBYLLA: I could be Bach, Brahms or Beethoven—I could be the next Nellie Melba and no-one would ever know—!

LUCY: You can't sing, Sybylla—

SYBYLLA: I have an unusual voice—

LUCY: Unusual, yes, beautiful, no—

SYBYLLA: [*singing*] The troubles of life are many,
The pleasures of life are few;
When we sat in the sunlight, Annie,
I dreamt that the skies were blue ... [1]

*Beat.*

LUCY: My old friends, the Milsons, are after a housemaid.

*Beat.*

[*Revealing a letter*] They're offering you a salary of ten pounds a year—

SYBYLLA: Mother ... *no*—

LUCY: There is no shame in service, Sybylla, it is good work, honest work—

SYBYLLA: It is a LIFE sentence—!

LUCY: [*indicating the baby*] *Keep* your voice down—

SYBYLLA: [*lowering volume, but not intensity*] You are handing me my judgement, and the judgement says: Sybylla Penelope Melvyn, you have served seven years on this barren ledge, / and in thanks and in gratitude, I will now HURL you off into outer darkness and oblivion!

LUCY: Oh, this is always the way ... I make a suggestion, it is

---

[1] From the poem *Wormwood and Nightshade* by Adam Lindsey Gordon (1867). Miles Franklin quotes Gordon's poetry throughout *My Brilliant Career.*

immediately put down, but no-one else cares to think of such things but me—

SYBYLLA: There are a *million* different things I could be—

LUCY: Name one. Name one trade or profession you have experience in—

SYBYLLA: Writing.

*Beat.*

LUCY: Oh … oh, Sybylla—

SYBYLLA: I won a prize—

LUCY: That was four years ago—

SYBYLLA: I came first in the *whole* school—

LUCY: There were *twenty-five* children in your school—!

SYBYLLA: It's not my fault I have inclinations towards better things. If I could be born again, I would, and I'd design myself the lowest stupidest coarsest-minded person imaginable so that I could find plenty of companionship in this *miserable* life—

LUCY: Then your quarrel is with God, it's not with me—

SYBYLLA: I don't believe there is a God—

LUCY: *Sybylla—!*

SYBYLLA: If he exists, he seems intent on torturing me for his own amusement—!

LUCY: What did I do to deserve a child as wicked as you—?

SYBYLLA: You married *him.*

*Silence. They stare at each other.*

LUCY: The hearth needs to be whitened. Then you can finish the pot lids. After that you can go and get your father—

SYBYLLA: I can't drag him out alone—!

LUCY: [*leaving*] So take your brother!

## *FIVE: ONCE A YEAR, EVERY YEAR*

RICHARD *stumbles home drunk.*

SYBYLLA *and* HORACE *trail behind him.*

HORACE: One hour.

One hour is all a cow needs … right?

Sometimes less.

She kicks her back legs, bellows a bit, and the whole thing just kind of … flops out … onto to the ground … blood and guts and all—

SYBYLLA: What's your point, Horace?

HORACE: When it's time for Ma to do the same, she takes a full day—*more*—and the screaming—you can hear that a mile away, so … so why's that then?

*Beat.*

SYBYLLA: Truth or fancy?

HORACE: Truth.

SYBYLLA: Ah, but convention would have me provide you with no warning at all— …

HORACE: *Truth.*

RICHARD *stops to relieve himself.*

SYBYLLA: One day, little brother, you will have a wife—

HORACE: Oh, no I bloody won't—!

SYBYLLA: You want me to tell you this, or not?

*Beat.* HORACE *nods.*

One day … you will have a wife. And on your wedding night, you will take off her clothes, and there you will see a body designed by God for gifting life, but not so well it won't curse her once a month or make her grip a kitchen table and scream. And once a year, every year, her little frame will belly out, and any one of those years, the babe inside might catch or shrivel up, might take your wifey too, and then everyone will gather round a little plot of earth and say things like, 'It was God's will', and, 'Return to your maker, little dove', and then, unable to take care of your own brood, you will claim yourself another younger wife, and the same game of risk and chance begins all over again—

HORACE: Stop it! You stop it now!

RICHARD *staggers on.*

SYBYLLA *and* HORACE *follow:* HORACE *kicking at things, grumbling.*

I'm going to be a bachelor.

Like Uncle Jay Jay.

I'm going to have a house in Sydney and a house in Melbourne too.

I'll go to parties, and theatre, I'll have lots of friends and I'll put babies in *none* of them.

And once a year, every year, I'll take a boat and go exploring. England. China. Russia. *America.* I'm going to see skyscrapers and and and prairie grass and—and *mountains*—covered in snow—!

SYBYLLA: No. You won't.

*Beat.*

You and I, Horace … we'll be lucky if we make it to Sydney … the *once*—

## *SIX: ESCAPE*

LUCY: Sybylla?

SYBYLLA *sits on a stool, milking a cow. Perhaps we hear the milk hit the tin pail with some dull monotonous rhythm.*

Sybylla—

SYBYLLA *continues.*

Sybylla—

*And again.*

I suppose you don't want to hear about this letter I've received? It's from your grandmother—

SYBYLLA: Grannie—!

LUCY: Sybylla—wait—!

SYBYLLA *launches herself at the letter, rips it out of her mother's hand.*

GRANDMA BOSSIER *(*GRANNIE*) appears.*

SYBYLLA: [*reading*] My dear daughter Lucy— / I am writing about Sybylla.

GRANNIE: I am writing about Sybylla. I am truly grieved to hear she is such a source of distress and annoyance to you. The girl must surely be ill or she would never act as you describe. Send her up to me as soon as you can, I will pay all expenses. Though she is young to mention in regard to marriage it might be the making of her if she married early. Gertie will soon be coming on, and Sybylla, being so very plain, will need all the help she can get.

GRANNIE *fades away.*

LUCY, *outed, shifts uncomfortably.*

SYBYLLA: **Three thoughts in furious succession: one, my mother had written to Grannie with a litany of my sins; two, I needed help to marry on account of being ugly; and three—**

LUCY: Sybylla, you know what Grannie's like. You mustn't pay any attention to—

SYBYLLA: **—Caddagat! I'm going to Caddagat!**

SYBYLLA *prepares to leave.*

**Goodbye, Possum Gully, with your narrow stagnating monotony!**

**Goodbye break-of-dawn milking, afternoon pig feeding and all-day poddy-rearing!**

**Goodbye snotty-nosed babies, your endless washing and your unrelenting cries!**

**Goodbye— …**

HORACE *and* GERTIE *appear.*

HORACE: It's not fair. It's not fair you get to go and I don't.

SYBYLLA: I'm the eldest—

HORACE: You're the worst. You get Ma all worked up and get rewarded for it too. And now I have to do all my work and yours so if you write me a letter, Syb, if you write me the longest letter, I won't read it, I'll scrunch it up and I'll *use* it. I'll use it on the bog—!

SYBYLLA: *Horace—!*

HORACE: [*leaving, tears smarting*] On the *bog,* Syb—so—so there.

HORACE *exits.*

GERTIE: It was your turn to set the table. But you didn't do it. So I did it. Only I told Ma that you did so there wouldn't be a row, and— … Are you ever coming back?

SYBYLLA: Not if I can help it.

GERTIE: What do I do when Horace makes fun of me? What will I say when Ma scolds me instead of you? What happens if Pa comes home drunk and no-one else is about—?

SYBYLLA: You put pondweed in Horace's bed. Ma would never scold you because you are irrefutably perfect. And if no-one's about, then lock the front door: you make Pa sleep in the yard, if you have to.

SYBYLLA *walks away.*

GERTIE: I love you, Sybylla. Better than anyone.

SYBYLLA *stops.*

SYBYLLA: **The love of a little sister is balm to a tempest-tossed soul.**

*She pauses as if to say something more, then thrusts her milk pail into* GERTIE*'s hands.*

BYE—!

*A flurry of movement.*

*SEVEN: FRANK HAWDEN*

*A train station.*

FRANK HAWDEN *enters.*

FRANK: Miss Melvyn? Miss Melvyn? I'm here to collect a Miss Sybylla Melvyn? Miss Melvyn, is that you?

SYBYLLA: Not remembering my birth, I can't swear; but I believe myself to be that same—!

FRANK: I'm Frank. Frank Hawden.

SYBYLLA: **Frank Hawden!**

FRANK: Recently from England.

SYBYLLA: **Recently from *England*! / Current overseer of Caddagat.**

FRANK: Current overseer of Caddagat.

*Beat.*

Well. I should smile.

SYBYLLA: And why is that, Mr Hawden?

FRANK: At you being the granddaughter of Mrs Bossier!

SYBYLLA: Oh?

FRANK: The niece of Mrs Helen Bell!

SYBYLLA: I fear, Mr Hawden, there's something the reverse of complimentary lurking in your remark.

FRANK: Would you like to have my opinion on you?

SYBYLLA: **Even if I didn't, I fear he would give it anyway—!**

FRANK: Well! You're neither a bit like Mrs Bossier or Mrs Bell because they are so good-looking.

SYBYLLA: Really!

FRANK: [*helping her into the cart*] I was a bit disappointed when I saw you have no pretentions to prettiness as there's not a girl up these parts worth wasting a man's affections on. I was building great hopes on you.

SYBYLLA: And how sorry I am to disappoint you.

FRANK: Never mind. Don't you worry yourself about that.

SYBYLLA: Indeed, Mr Hawden … I won't!

*As they drive,* FRANK *chatters away to himself, oblivious to the fact that* SYBYLLA *is speaking to the audience. Over this, day turns to dusky twilight and Caddagat materialises.*

| | |
|---|---|
| FRANK: It's only an hour or so from here—see, the river on our right? Just there—through the shrubbery. | SYBYLLA: **… how familiar were all the landmarks!** |
| And that line of trees over there—that's Five Bob Downs—see? Away over that range. Five Bob Downs belongs to Mr Harold Beecham—it's a fine station—a very fine station indeed—oh, but I suppose you know the places better than I do, seeing as you used to live here—! | **… the sweet sad rush of mountain waters … the ferny gullies … swarming with lyrebirds … the white mists brought by the rain curling down the hills and—** **… [*looking up*] … oh!** |
| *The birds begin screeching.* | **… the skreel of a hundred curlews—!** |
| My my my, oh my! That's a horrible racket, isn't it? Where I'm from, the birds have the good sense to sound like actual | **… wild *hunted* spirits …** |

<table>
<tr><td>birds as opposed to a giant pig being slaughtered—Christ!—there they go again—!</td><td>… how I love their lonely wail!<br>… and there …</td></tr>
<tr><td>SHUT UP—SHUT UP—SHUT UP—you just have to yell at them a bit, Miss Melvyn, and generally they do defer …</td><td>… peeping out a mass of greenery and fruit …</td></tr>
<tr><td>… ooo, almost there, see, Miss Melvyn?<br>Over there …</td><td>… the place where I was born …</td></tr>
<tr><td>… that's the front gate of Caddagat.</td><td>… Caddagat!</td></tr>
</table>

GRANNIE *and* AUNT HELEN *emerge from the darkness.*

## *EIGHT: CADDAGAT*

GRANNIE: Helen!

SYBYLLA: **Grandma Bossier.**

GRANNIE: Helen, they've arrived!

SYBYLLA: **Long-time widow and formidable forewoman of Caddagat.**

**And Aunt Helen Bell. Married to a man whose absence has never been sufficiently explained.**

**How will they greet me? Poor, penniless girl-child, source of distress to her mother, no pretentions to prettiness— …!**

GRANNIE *folds* SYBYLLA *into an enormous hug.*

GRANNIE: My dear dear child. How I have missed you.

AUNT HELEN: Welcome, Sybylla. We're so glad to have a young person about to brighten the place.

GRANNIE: [*putting on her wrap*] But you'll have to forgive me, Sybylla. Mrs Wilshaw has decided tonight is the night to have her baby, so you and I, we shall have our reunion over breakfast …

*She pauses with the lamp over* SYBYLLA*'s face.*

… not a bit like your mother, are you? Never mind. You have beautiful hair, and there's nothing I admire so much as a good head of hair— [*leaving*] —Frank! —sleep well, Sybylla.

*She exits with* FRANK.

AUNT HELEN: Come. I'll take you to your room.

*They move through the house.*

I do hope you like it. I arranged it on purpose to suit you—

SYBYLLA: Oh … Aunt!

SYBYLLA *stops at a portrait or photograph.*

Isn't she *lovely*! It's you, isn't it?

AUNT HELEN: Me? Don't you recognise your own mother? This was Lucy's room when she was your age. That likeness was made just before her marriage.

*As* AUNT HELEN *continues chatting,* SYBYLLA *moves towards the portrait.*

You'll notice the basket of apples in the corner. Harry Beecham brought them over this afternoon, hoping, I'm sure, to catch a look at you. Young ladies are in the minority up here, so I suspect it's the first fruit basket of many and— [*turning*] … Sybylla … are you— … are you / crying—?

SYBYLLA: No—sorry—it's nothing—really—

AUNT HELEN: Please, tell me—

SYBYLLA: No, it doesn't bear voicing—

AUNT HELEN: It must be hard to leave your mother, your little brothers and sisters— …?

SYBYLLA: I am UGLY, Aunt Helen, so you'd better warn Harry Beecham and everyone else!

*Beat.*

AUNT HELEN: Ugly? Sybylla … you're no such thing—

SYBYLLA: [*motioning towards the mirror*] I am *disgusting.* My nose is too small, my forehead is *extremely* large, and as if that wasn't burden enough, I have developed a reputation for *cleverness*, which puts me out of matrimonial running as effectually as if I had developed *leprosy*—!

AUNT HELEN: Sybylla—

SYBYLLA: From this *very* room, my father stole my mother away—and to what?! Endless work—unavailing poverty! *This* is life as proved by my mother—and *she*—beautiful! What right do I have to expect a better yield—!

AUNT HELEN: [*turning her from the mirror*] Oh, my dear girl! I would never dream of calling you plain, let alone ugly …

SYBYLLA: That's not to say I'm not—

AUNT HELEN: You're not—

SYBYLLA: When compliments are almost reservedly about one's hair—?

AUNT HELEN: And it's *wonderful* hair. But it's not your only quality, I assure you.

*She takes* SYBYLLA*'s hand, tries to coax a smile.*

Come, Sybylla. I have a plan …

## *NINE: AUNT HELEN'S RECIPES*

*As* SYBYLLA *speaks, she is transformed.*

SYBYLLA: **Every morning, Aunt Helen insists I observe a number of unimpeachable rites:**

AUNT HELEN: The washing of one's hands, feet, and face, Sybylla, is a *twice* daily ritual, *not* to be ignored

SYBYLLA: **Baths, however**

AUNT HELEN: twice a week

SYBYLLA: **in warm soapy water not previously used by seven siblings**

AUNT HELEN: and onion juice

SYBYLLA: **diluted and massaged through the scalp and hair**

AUNT HELEN: and then dried and dressed—Mary will show you how.

MARY O'FARRELL, *the Bossier's Irish housemaid, enters and dresses* SYBYLLA*'s hair.*

SYBYLLA: **During this time, I am not allowed to encroach upon the contents of the bookshelf—Byron, Thackeray, Dickens!—how I long to clasp hands with them in friendship, but instead am given**

MARY: [*passing a hairbrush*] One hundred strokes at night, Miss Melvyn, and every night. I can help you with it if you like?

SYBYLLA: **And though Aunt Helen prefers I stay inside, if I must venture out**

AUNT HELEN: gloves, parasol, a shady hat

SYBYLLA: **until my farm-burnt skin blanches to an acceptable hue.**

AUNT HELEN: [*with powder*] Nothing garish. Just a subtle enhancement of your natural features

SYBYLLA: **which she covers entirely in powder, blush and paint, and finally …**

AUNT HELEN *brings out a beautiful evening dress.*

AUNT HELEN: All the way from Sydney.

SYBYLLA *traces the dress with her fingers.*

SYBYLLA: Sydney …

AUNT HELEN: The colour, I think, will be most becoming.

AUNT HELEN *dresses* SYBYLLA.

Are you ready, Sybylla?

SYBYLLA *nods and* AUNT HELEN *turns or uncovers the mirror.*

SYBYLLA *stares at herself.*

*And stares at herself.*

*And stares at herself.*

Well? What do you think?

SYBYLLA: I think … I think …

AUNT HELEN: … Yes?

SYBYLLA: I think evening dress is one of the most idiotic customs extant—!

AUNT HELEN: Right— …

SYBYLLA: What can be more foolish than exposing both the chest AND the arms in the cold air of night?! On the other hand … there are many who have chest and arms that will not admit to being displayed, but mine are *hungry* for want of use, and now that I discovered you, I will put you on *violent* display … oh, yes I will—!

AUNT HELEN: Sybylla, I wonder— …? Does every thought of yours *need* to be articulated?

SYBYLLA: But— … I have so many—?

AUNT HELEN: And there are other girls—as clever as you—who have learnt to use this intelligence—

SYBYLLA: *Use* it—?

AUNT HELEN: —to hide the fact of its existence.

Think as much as you like, my dear. And when you feel that wildness of spirit surging somewhere within you … take a deep breath … count to three or five or ten, if you have to, then ask yourself:

… 'Can I do any good by giving this voice?'

*Pause.*

SYBYLLA: Thank you for this dress, Aunt.

AUNT HELEN: You're very welcome.

*TEN: A NEW POSSIBILITY*

UNCLE JAY JAY: Where is she?! Where's my little mischief-monkey!

SYBYLLA: **Julius John Bossier.**

UNCLE JAY JAY: By George! Who's this wonderful-looking girl?

SYBYLLA: **My mother's brother.**

UNCLE JAY JAY: And this hair! I'll give the next shearer who passes a shilling to cut it all off—it'd kill a dog in winter—give us a kiss then—

SYBYLLA: Uncle Jay Jay! You smell of whisky and tobacco!

UNCLE JAY JAY: But that's what makes my kisses taste so nice!

GRANNIE: [*entering*] Julius, your conduct, as ever, leaves something to be desired—

UNCLE JAY JAY: Nonsense, Mother! I bet you were often kissed when that youngster's age—now confess.

*Beat.*

GRANNIE: I was. It's true.

UNCLE JAY JAY: My mother! The harlot wench!

GRANNIE: Not in front of the servants, Julius.

UNCLE JAY JAY: Servant, Mother. Singular. Mary, you don't mind working for a known *debauchée,* / do you—?

GRANNIE: Julius!

MARY: [*bored*] No, Mr Bossier, I can't say I do—

UNCLE JAY JAY: See, Mother! Wench, away! You have Mary O'Farrell's express approval! Frank Hawden, lurking in the background again, I see—

FRANK: Well, I—

UNCLE JAY JAY: You've met my niece, Sybylla, have you not?

FRANK: Well, I—

UNCLE JAY JAY: Sybylla, I can say without a fragment of doubt: Frank Hawden is the most profoundly acceptable overseer we've ever had.

FRANK: [*chuffed*] Well, that is the highest compliment anyone has ever paid me!

UNCLE JAY JAY: [*pouring him a drink*] Frank, I do believe that, I really do.

FRANK: Miss Sybylla, you look *wonderful* tonight.

SYBYLLA: Do I, Frank?

FRANK: As vibrant as the rich and tangled vines which adorn your bedroom window …

GRANNIE: Mr Hawden has an interest in writing, did you know that, Sybylla?

FRANK: I dabble a bit, it's true.

GRANNIE: He's always coming up with the most wonderful turns of phrase—!

FRANK: [*pretend embarrassed*] Mrs Bossier—!

GRANNIE: Perhaps you'd like to share something, Frank—?

FRANK: [*searching his pockets*] Well, I— … I haven't really anything prepared—?

UNCLE JAY JAY: Don't worry yourself then, Frank—

FRANK: [*finding something*] Oh—no—I do! My poem is called—

UNCLE JAY JAY: Can you do anything interesting, Sybylla?

*Beat.*

SYBYLLA: Excuse me?

UNCLE JAY JAY: There's no point having a pretty young woman 'bout the place if she can't entertain us, so please, someone tell me she can sing?

AUNT HELEN: She sings very nicely by herself sometimes, but I'm not sure how she'd manage with an— [audience] …

*But* SYBYLLA *is already at the piano, pounding a few simple chords and singing at the top of her lungs.*

SYBYLLA: [*singing*] The troubles of life are many
The pleasures of life are few
When we sat in the sunlight, Annie,
I dreamt that the skies were blue—
When we sat in the sunlight, Annie—
I dreamt that the earth was green
There is little colour, if any
'Neath the sunlight now to be seen!

UNCLE JAY JAY *goes to the bookshelf and takes down a copy of 'The Taming of the Shrew'.* FRANK, *seizing his opportunity:*

FRANK: My poem is called—

UNCLE JAY JAY: [*to* SYBYLLA] Read from this—

MARY: Ma'am, I'm sorry, dinner's already on the table—

GRANNIE: Julius—

UNCLE JAY JAY: [*reciting from memory*] —You lie, in faith, for you are call'd plain Kate!— [*speeding through*] —ahhh, something something something—myself am moved to woo thee for my wife!'

SYBYLLA: [*reading*] 'Moved! In good time: let him that moved you hither
Remove you hence: I knew you at the first
You were a moveable.'

UNCLE JAY JAY: Why, what's a moveable?

SYBYLLA: A join'd-stool.

UNCLE JAY JAY: Thou hast hit it: come, sit on me.

SYBYLLA: Asses are made to bear, and so are you.

UNCLE JAY JAY: Women are made to bear, and so are you.

SYBYLLA: No such jade as you, if me you mean.

UNCLE JAY JAY: Alas! Good Kate, I will not burden thee,
For, knowing thee to be but young and light—

SYBYLLA: Too light for such a swain as you to catch,
And yet as heavy as my weight should be.

*Beat.*

FRANK: 'The Green Grass of England'.

The grass of England is very green,
The greenest grass I've ever seen—

UNCLE JAY JAY: Do you have any accents, Sybylla?

*Beat.*

SYBYLLA: Accents?

UNCLE JAY JAY: Can you mimic, girl—!

SYBYLLA: [*Uncle Jay Jay*] Can you mimic, girl—!

UNCLE JAY JAY: Frank's turn—!

FRANK: Oh … no need—

SYBYLLA: [*Frank*] The Green Grass of England. The grass of England / is very green—

FRANK: —is very green—!

UNCLE JAY JAY: Mary! Do Mary—!

SYBYLLA: [*Mary*] Ma'am, I'm sorry, dinner's already on the table—

UNCLE JAY JAY: Wasn't that *marvellous*, Mary!

MARY: [*without emotion*] Yes, sir. A perfect capture.

UNCLE JAY JAY: Do you know, Mother, I think you may be robbing the world of an artist by keeping her locked away in the bush—?

SYBYLLA: / Me?!

AUNT HELEN: Now, Jay Jay—

GRANNIE: An artist?

UNCLE JAY JAY: I must persuade you to let me take her up to Sydney—

SYBYLLA: / Sydney!

AUNT HELEN: / Sydney!

GRANNIE: Whatever for?!

UNCLE JAY JAY: I'll bear the expense myself—elocution lessons—singing—only the best masters—!

GRANNIE: But what would she do with that kind of training—?

UNCLE JAY JAY: Why, go on the stage of course—

SYBYLLA: / The stage!

AUNT HELEN: / The stage?

GRANNIE: The stage! A granddaughter of mine?!

UNCLE JAY JAY: With all her talent and hair she could be quite the sensation—!

GRANNIE: Her father may be a lout, Julius, but she is still the child of a respectable family—

UNCLE JAY JAY: Mother, acting is a perfectly reasonable profession—

GRANNIE: It is defiled in the sight of God! Do you know the kind of people, who become actresses—?

UNCLE JAY JAY: Who—?

GRANNIE: Hussies! Vile, low, brazen hussies! I would rather my eyelids closed in *death* before I see my Sybylla on a *stage*—

UNCLE JAY JAY: [*nudging* SYBYLLA] Not long to wait then—!

GRANNIE: Enough. No more talk of that. Now. Next autumn, when the fruit picking and jam making are done, Helen can take the child to Sydney and perhaps, Julius, you can show them around—

UNCLE JAY JAY: [*whispering to* SYBYLLA] And should we meet a few personal friends who happen to be leading managers of theatres—?

GRANNIE: [*leaving for dinner*] I'm old, Julius, I'm not deaf!

SYBYLLA: **Acting! Why hadn't I thought of it before?! True, I had never seen a play, nor read one until tonight, but a sudden thought took hold of me …**

**… I could do it, and *well*—**

*ELEVEN: A LETTER TO GERTIE*

SYBYLLA: **Dearest Gertie,**

**I have started to write no less than seven letters to you but I will endeavour to finish this and will parenthesise all interruptions!**

AUNT HELEN *plays the piano.*

**Living here is LOVELY!**

AUNT HELEN: Come, Sybylla, listen to this …

SYBYLLA: **The world is FULL of good and love, and I am COMPLETE mistress of it! Here, there are very few duties allotted to me …**

GRANNIE: Fresh fruit, my dear.

SYBYLLA: **One of these is to help Grannie with the accounts and to write extremely forceful business letters—**

GRANNIE: [*reading*] 'In light of your repeated disregard / for the principal constituents of basic commerce—'

SYBYLLA: [*overlapping*] —for the principal constituents of basic commerce—

GRANNIE: —oh, Sybylla, this is *very* good.

SYBYLLA: **Another is to take elocution and deportment lessons from Uncle Jay Jay—**

UNCLE JAY JAY: [*placing a book on her head*] Straight back, Sybylla, eyes to the front—

SYBYLLA: **—parts of which, Grannie has approved, and others she most certainly has not—**

UNCLE JAY JAY: [*flipping this same book open*] Oh, you kind Gods—!

SYBYLLA: [*an overwrought Cordelia*] Oh, you kind Gods! Cure this great breach in his abused nature—!

TRAMP: Spare a bit of food, miss?

SYBYLLA: **And finally, I attend to the tramps.**

*This sequence could involve one or more than one 'tramp'.*

TRAMP: Loaf of bread will do.

TRAMP: Chew of tobacco, even better.

SYBYLLA: **What a great army they are, Gertie! We feed, on average, fifty tramps a week and never see the same man twice—**

MARY: [*handing out the supplies*] Flour, beef, tobacco, tea. And an extra blanket to keep you warm. You can sleep behind the sheds if you like, it'll be cold tonight.

TRAMP: Thank you, miss.

TRAMP: God bless your pleasant face.

SYBYLLA *watches the* TRAMP(S) *depart, another letter to Gertie forgotten.*

SYBYLLA: You know, if we stopped feeding them all—charged board and lodging instead, we'd make my uncle a pretty fortune …

MARY: Is that right?

SYBYLLA: We'd be doing them a favour really; they need to learn—

MARY: Learn what?

SYBYLLA: To work for their food—

MARY: Ah. Like your uncle does.

UNCLE JAY JAY *is sunning himself outside.*

SYBYLLA: Mary, my uncle travels to Sydney almost every week—

MARY: Forgive me, Miss Melvyn—

SYBYLLA: —on *many* important business matters—

MARY: Of course—

SYBYLLA: So why do I always suspect there are a million different meanings in what you say—?

MARY: Oh, I hardly know what I mean most of the time—

SYBYLLA: Mary.

*Beat.*

MARY: Did you ever wonder why the Beechams called that big estate Five Bob Downs?

SYBYLLA: Some kind of private joke, I imagine?

MARY: It's how much they paid for it. Back in the day. What do you think five bob will get you now?

SYBYLLA: Oh, I don't know—

MARY: That dress. I'd say that dress cost about five bob. Usually, it would cost significantly more, only in this case, the seamstress wasn't paid to make it—that—that was part of my salary—do you know how much a housemaid makes, Miss Melvyn—?

SYBYLLA: [*she does*] Ten pounds a year.

*Pause. They stare at each other.*

MARY: Can't buy a piece of land on that. Not anymore. Now, can I leave the rest of these supplies for you to hand out, or …

*But a new thought is rapidly forming in* SYBYLLA*'s mind.*

… Miss? … Miss Sybylla—?

SYBYLLA: Why don't we do something about it?

*Beat.*

MARY: … I'm sorry—?

SYBYLLA: Mary, why don't we all just—just—just rise up—

MARY: / Rise up—?

SYBYLLA: —against injustice, and—and tyranny—and—and exploitation—?!

MARY: Because after this your grandmother wants me to finish the polishing—

SYBYLLA: **I'm going to be a political radical.**

*Beat.*

MARY: Miss Sybylla—?

SYBYLLA: **I am going to be what Grannie calls 'a dreadful female agitator—'**

MARY: Miss Sybylla, please, if you're not going to help me with this—

SYBYLLA: **I am going to hold a placard, and hand out leaflets, and shout at people in the street—!**

MARY: Fine. I suppose I'm doing it myself then—

SYBYLLA: **I will be fierce, and eccentric, and lonely—no—no, I won't be lonely because I will have *Mary*—**

MARY: [*gathering the supplies*] Ten pounds isn't nearly enough for this shite—

SYBYLLA: **—and together, we will travel the country—**

*MARY sings to herself as she leaves. SYBYLLA continues, oblivious to MARY's exit.*

MARY: [*singing*]
An old man came courting
me, hey ding doorum dah
An old man came courting
me, me being young
An old man came courting
me …[2]

SYBYLLA:
**—sleeping in ditches—
making speeches—
harassing local
dignitaries—heeding the cry
of the millions oppressed,
downtrodden, God-forsaken
…** Mary, together we could
rearrange the WORLD—!

*TWELVE: UNWANTED ADVANCES*

FRANK: Ah! Miss Melvyn! Fancy finding you here.

*SYBYLLA, dazed.*

I suppose you're rehearsing some more of those accents to show off with tonight?

SYBYLLA: No. No, Mary and I were just …

*She notices MARY has gone.*

Mary—?

FRANK: If a girl is disengaged, any man has the right to pay his addresses—

---

[2] 'An Old Man Came Courting Me' or 'Never Wed an Old Man' (1867), a popular Irish song.

SYBYLLA: But I'm not— … I'm not disengaged—

FRANK: Of course, convention would have you make some attempt to discourage me—

SYBYLLA: But I'm not disengaged—

FRANK: I do enjoy a challenge.

*Beat.*

Where on earth did you learn to sing? Such depth, such warmth—!

SYBYLLA: Mr Hawden, please—

FRANK: I love you.

*Beat.*

SYBYLLA: Excuse me—?

FRANK: I love you. I have feelings. And the feelings I have are—

SYBYLLA: Mr Hawden, name one thing you know about me.

*Beat.*

Just one.

FRANK: You're uh …

SYBYLLA: Yes?

FRANK: Why, you're the granddaughter of Mrs Bossier, the niece of Mrs Helen Bell—

SYBYLLA: Beyond the obvious, Mr Hawden.

FRANK: You looked wonderful in that dress—?

SYBYLLA: The dress—?

FRANK: Yes, the one you wore the other night.

SYBYLLA: Are you sure it's not the dress that appeals then?

FRANK: Well, of course it appeals—didn't I just say—?

SYBYLLA: [*trying to leave*] Then why don't we give Aunt Helen your measurements and she'll send for one in your size—no need to hanker after mine—

FRANK: [*blocking her path*] My God, you are *wild*—

SYBYLLA: Mr Hawden—

FRANK: I'd love to take you home to England—by Jove!—you'd surprise some English girls I know—

SYBYLLA: [*still trying to leave*] Mr Hawden—

FRANK: Frank—

SYBYLLA: [*still trying to leave*] Mr Hawden—

FRANK: My love, I really must insist you call me Frank—

SYBYLLA: And I too must insist: if you have any sense of personal dignity then please, Mr Hawden, stop persecuting me with these professions of love!

*Beat.*

FRANK: My dear, I have— … I have asked quite a few times that you call me Frank?

*Out of sheer frustration,* SYBYLLA *exclaims, turns, takes a deep breath, begins to count.*

… Miss Melvyn—?

SYBYLLA: One, two, three, four, five … [*etc*]

FRANK: [*overlapping*] Are you— … are you are you quite alright, or—?

SYBYLLA: [*trying to leave*] If I stay any longer, Mr Hawden, I worry you'll find out—

FRANK: Oh, you won't escape me, plain Kate, for I myself am moved to woo thee for a wife—!

*He grabs her,* SYBYLLA *whirls around, knocks him to the floor.*

SYBYLLA: How *dare* you!

*Beat.*

FRANK: I— … I beg your pardon—

SYBYLLA: If you ever touch me again, Mr Hawden, I'll give you a bloody nose, I promise you!

*A terrible silence.*

*Then* FRANK *smiles.*

*Holds her in his gaze.*

FRANK: You *hideous* little barbarian.

*Beat.*

You seem to think that just because Grannie has a little money it makes a lady of you. Oh, Miss Melvyn … nothing could be further from the truth.

FRANK, *away.*

GRANNIE: Sybylla—

*THIRTEEN: A GREATER PURPOSE YET*

UNCLE JAY JAY *lounges about nearby, reading his newspaper.*

GRANNIE: —it grieves me that any young man should have to speak to me about the behaviour of my own granddaughter.

*Beat.*

SYBYLLA: And what did Mr Hawden have to say—?

GRANNIE: He says you have been flirting with him. He says you have been forward. Bold. Brazen. Immodest. And … *unwomanly.*

SYBYLLA: Is that everything?

GRANNIE: No. He wants to marry you and has asked my consent.

SYBYLLA: / What?

UNCLE JAY JAY: [*putting his newspaper away and settling in*] Good God, I can't wait for this.

SYBYLLA: *Marry* him? Marry that *boy*?!

GRANNIE: He's no boy, Sybylla. Frank has attained his majority and in less than a year will be in possession of quite a substantial property—

SYBYLLA: He's an *idiot*—!

GRANNIE: Yes. He is. But he also has a great deal of money. It's a good match, Sybylla, you'd do well to accept—

SYBYLLA: And what if I don't want to?

GRANNIE: My dear, outside of my good name, you're neither rich in funds nor prospects—

SYBYLLA: What if I don't intend to marry at all?

*Beat.*

GRANNIE: Well, that's simply not an option—

SYBYLLA: But Grannie—

GRANNIE: If you don't marry you will lose all respectability. Your peers will shun you, your father and mother will be burdened with your care—and when they depart from this life—which poor brother of yours will have to support you—?

SYBYLLA: I'll find a career; I'll support myself—!

GRANNIE: You'll do no such thing. God didn't create women to eke out a living, Sybylla. He made us for love. And motherhood. And, in this part of the world, I believe, God made us for a greater purpose yet—

UNCLE JAY JAY: Brace yourself, Sybylla—

GRANNIE: It is our God-given duty to replenish this land and hold it from the peril at our doors—

SYBYLLA: The peril—?

GRANNIE: Foreigners—!

UNCLE JAY JAY: Ah—there it is—

GRANNIE: *Clamouring* to get in! Every man has three wives, every wife has ten children—they produce at the rate of rabbits—!

SYBYLLA: Your own daughter has eight children and counting—

GRANNIE: And well she should. To steady us against the swarm—

SYBYLLA: The *swarm*—?

GRANNIE: This land can only sustain so many people—

SYBYLLA: Then perhaps we should all unite against our husbands—stop the swarming business entirely!

GRANNIE: Sybylla. If I had spoken to my own grandmother this way, I would have been locked up on bread and water.

SYBYLLA: Better that than marriage with *Frank Hawden*—

GRANNIE: *Sybylla*—

SYBYLLA: Better that than marriage with anyone—!

GRANNIE: Are you going to say something, Julius, or are you just going to / sit there—

UNCLE JAY JAY: Sit here and enjoy it, Mother, thank you for asking—

SYBYLLA: Marriage to even the best man in the world, Grannie, is a lowering thing—

GRANNIE: It is a *sacred* institution—

SYBYLLA: Designed by man to clamp us down—!

GRANNIE: *Enough*—

SYBYLLA: And what good has population done anyway—?!

GRANNIE: I said, *enough*—!

SYBYLLA: —except to spoil this part of the earth—?!

GRANNIE: GO. You can pick me some lemons from the orchard—!

SYBYLLA, *wrapped in dirty work clothes, begins to climb.*

SYBYLLA: [*shouting down*] *We* are the swarm, Grannie! *We* are the swarm—!

GRANNIE: [*shouting up*] —and when you are ready to apologise to Mr Hawden, and then to myself, you can come back—!

SYBYLLA: Oh, I will *never* marry! I will never marry! I will never never never never never never—!

*FOURTEEN: ... HE*

SYBYLLA *is up a tree, picking lemons, singing Mary's song.*

SYBYLLA: [*singing, accented*] … never wed an old man.
Because he's got no faloorum, fal-liddy-i-oorum
He's got no faloorum fal-diddy di daa
He's got no faloorum he's lost his ding doorum
Maids, when you're young never wed an old man …

HAROLD BEECHAM *has wandered into the orchard.* SYBYLLA *notices, far too late, that he's watching her. She freezes.*

HAROLD: Hello there.

*Beat.*

Please—don't stop. I'm used to hearing that song in the shearing sheds, but never from a woman, and never … never up a tree …

*Beat.*

I'm Harold.

SYBYLLA: **Harry Beecham!**

HAROLD: Harold Beecham.

SYBYLLA: **Giver of apples. Owner of Five Bob Downs.**

HAROLD: Fine by me if you don't want to engage in conversation. Happy to just rest here a while … [*looking up her skirt*] ... admire the view …

SYBYLLA *swings her skirt over herself, attempts to climb down the tree.* HAROLD *grips her by the waist and 'helps' her down.*

Well now … Mrs Bossier always knows how to pick a maid: can manage the job, I'm sure, but I'll bet you provide some spectacle while doing it …

SYBYLLA: [*affecting a thick Irish accent*] If you please, sir. I need to be getting back—

HAROLD: Not until you give me a kiss—
SYBYLLA: Oh no, the missus might catch me …
HAROLD: I'll take the blame if she does—
SYBYLLA: No—Mr Beecham—please—
HAROLD: Come back here—
SYBYLLA: I said NO.

*He stops.*

HAROLD: Alright. No need to get upset. I never kiss anyone against their will—was just having a bit of fun, that's all—
SYBYLLA: Fun—?
HAROLD: Yes. Let's have some more. Stand out there. I want to see if you've got any grit in you.

SYBYLLA *moves to where he points and waits.* HAROLD *uncurls his whip, and then, with a great deal of skill (but also pretension) cracks it neatly near her face.*

SYBYLLA *doesn't even flinch.*

HAROLD *lowers his whip, intrigued.*

SYBYLLA *grins and runs for it.*

Wait! What's your name?

## *FIFTEEN: OLD FRIENDS*

GRANNIE: … The cost of merging six separate colonies, Harry—six separate governments! Untangling that mess of law and trade …
UNCLE JAY JAY: Law and trade? What about travel first! We still can't get from Sydney to Melbourne without changing trains at the border.
GRANNIE: All that new infrastructure, we'll see it in our taxes, you mark my words …
HAROLD: We may not see Federation at all. Western Australia still doesn't want to join. They think they're stronger alone.
UNCLE JAY JAY: Blast them!
GRANNIE: Language, Julius— …
UNCLE JAY JAY: We'll take New Zealand instead.
HAROLD: New Zealand doesn't want to join either.
UNCLE JAY JAY: Well, blast them too—!

GRANNIE: Julius!

UNCLE JAY JAY: See how long they fare floating alone in the South Pacific—I certainly won't be throwing them a buoy—

SYBYLLA *enters, almost unnoticed.*

—ah, Sybylla!

SYBYLLA *is decked out in full evening dress.*

HAROLD *turns. Can barely contain his shock.*

GRANNIE: Harry, this is my granddaughter, Sybylla. She's the one you've been collecting all those apples for.

SYBYLLA: Mr Beecham.

*She extends her hand for* HAROLD *to kiss.*

HAROLD: Miss Melvyn.

UNCLE JAY JAY: So formal! You'd think the two of you had never met!

HAROLD: Where have we …?

UNCLE JAY JAY: You used to play together as children—

HAROLD: Did we—?

UNCLE JAY JAY: Oh yes, Sybylla used to murder you repeatedly on the front lawn. What was that she used to call you—Paddy—Piggy—?

SYBYLLA: [*realising*] Podgy— …

UNCLE JAY JAY: Podgy! That's it. Little Podgy!

HAROLD: Yes, I uh … I think I remember something of that.

SYBYLLA *smiles at* HAROLD. HAROLD *can barely hold her gaze for the embarrassment.*

GRANNIE: Julius. I suspect Helen might need some help in the kitchen … shall we go check on her?

UNCLE JAY JAY: What the blazes would I do in a kitchen?

GRANNIE: I'm sure we can find you something—

UNCLE JAY JAY: I don't even know where it is—! [*Nudging* HAROLD, *laughing*] Isn't that right, Harold—?

GRANNIE: Then you better come with me, Julius, and I'll show you exactly.

*Beat.* UNCLE JAY JAY *puts down his glass and exits.*

*Once alone:*

HAROLD: Miss Melvyn … I must say, I had no idea it was you.

SYBYLLA: So it's fine to have your fun at the expense of a housemaid?

HAROLD: I can assure you that was entirely out of character—

SYBYLLA: You can't deceive me now, Mr Beecham. I know exactly the kind of character you are—

HAROLD: And I you. You had no right to dress and talk like that, misleading a fellow—

SYBYLLA: Then perhaps we should divulge all to Grandmother in order to redeem both our characters—?

HAROLD: No!

*Beat.*

No. No, I'm uh … I'm happy to keep quiet about it if you are? … A secret?

SYBYLLA: A secret?

HAROLD: Between two old friends?

*He extends his hand. She shakes it.*

Wonderful to be reacquainted with you, Miss Melvyn.

SYBYLLA: And I with you, Mr Beecham.

## *SIXTEEN: AUNT HELEN'S STORY*

SYBYLLA: **This was Thursday. The following Saturday, Sunday and Tuesday, Harold Beecham appears at Caddagat again. We sit by the fire and Mr Beecham interposes—**

HAROLD: Yes.

SYBYLLA: **and**

HAROLD: No.

SYBYLLA: **at the proper intervals in Grannie's brisk business conversation, but never addresses one word to me beyond—**

HAROLD: Good afternoon, Miss Melvyn.

SYBYLLA: **on arrival and**

HAROLD: Good evening, Miss Melvyn.

SYBYLLA: **on departure.**

SYBYLLA *fires questions at* AUNT HELEN *who is in the middle of frantic cooking (or some such).*

Aunt Helen, does Harold Beecham ever talk any more than that?

AUNT HELEN: Often a great deal less—

SYBYLLA: How old is he?

AUNT HELEN: Twenty-one last December—

SYBYLLA: Did he ever have any brothers and sisters?

AUNT HELEN: No, his birth caused his mother's death—

SYBYLLA: His father?

AUNT HELEN: Died before Harry could crawl—

SYBYLLA: So who raised him—?

AUNT HELEN: His Aunt Augusta—

SYBYLLA: Is Five Bob a very pretty place—?

AUNT HELEN: And why would you like to know—?

SYBYLLA: I'm only asking because—

AUNT HELEN: He's a good boy, Sybylla, but he does have a reputation—

SYBYLLA: I believe it! He's *very* conceited—!

AUNT HELEN: All that money, he can have any girl for the asking— …

SYBYLLA: I'll surprise him if he thinks he can get me—!

AUNT HELEN: Sybylla, I— … I need to tell you something. And if my experience can serve in any way as warning—

SYBYLLA: Is this something to do with your husband?

*Beat.*

AUNT HELEN: What do you know of my husband?

SYBYLLA: Only that no-one ever talks of him.

*Beat.*

Is he— … is he dead—?

AUNT HELEN: What—?

SYBYLLA: He's dead, isn't he—? Oh, God—how awful for you—! A dead husband—!

AUNT HELEN: He's not *dead*, Sybylla, he's— …

SYBYLLA: What?

*Pause.*

AUNT HELEN: My husband … Colonel Bell … lives in America. I did too. For a short while. That is. Until.

*Beat.*

He tried to obtain a divorce—

SYBYLLA: A *divorce*—?!

AUNT HELEN: It was my own fault, Sybylla, I married the man three weeks after meeting him—less than a year later, he— … he met someone else. But a divorce was unconscionable for me—for—for Mother—so I agreed to return home—

SYBYLLA: And still married?

AUNT HELEN: In name, at least—

SYBYLLA: At *least*—?

AUNT HELEN: Sybylla, a divorced woman has no respectable place in society—

SYBYLLA: But what if you want to marry again—?

AUNT HELEN: Listen to me—*please*— / I—I want you to know love, Sybylla, I do—but I want you to know the kind of love that grows *softly*—over—over many—many years—

SYBYLLA: [*overlapping*] You're younger than my mother! You could have children yet if you wanted them! You could be head of your own home—your own LIFE—not stuck here—*branded* with his name—cooking and cleaning for your mother and brother until your dying days—at least Mary is *paid*—!

AUNT HELEN: *STOP.*

*Her raised voice shocks them both.*

I'm— … I'm sorry, I— … I shouldn't— … I shouldn't have raised my voice—

SYBYLLA: Aunt—

AUNT HELEN: I don't want to talk on this particular topic anymore—

SYBYLLA: But—

AUNT HELEN: I want to talk about you, and— … and Harry—

SYBYLLA: Oh, Aunt, as we've already established, Harold Beecham can have any girl for the asking—!

AUNT HELEN: And he's asking you. [*Revealing a letter*] I received a letter from his Aunt Augusta. She wonders if you might like to stay a while at Five Bob?

*Beat.*

Of course … if you don't want to go—?

SYBYLLA: [*taking the letter*] No! No, it uh … it might be nice to see the famous Five Bob Downs …?

*Beat.*

AUNT HELEN: Well. We must see about getting you some more dresses then—!

SYBYLLA: Aunt Helen?

You didn't do anything wrong.

*Beat.*

You don't need to punish yourself.

*A moment.*

*And just as quickly,* AUNT HELEN *closes herself back up.*

AUNT HELEN: And a new hat!

*SEVENTEEN: FIVE BOB DOWNS*

*As* SYBYLLA *talks, she's furnished with a new dress and very big hat.*

SYBYLLA: **If you consider Caddagat a kind of Eden then Five Bob Downs is surely the Sweet Hereafter. Dreamy blue hills bordering wide rich flats leading to a six-acre flower garden surrounding a broad verandah attached to a great spreading house—!**

AUNT AUGUSTA: Sybylla Penelope Melvyn.

SYBYLLA: **Harry's Aunt Augusta.**

AUNT AUGUSTA: The last time I saw you, you weren't a scrap above three feet.

SYBYLLA: **Member of the dreaded 'Spinsterhood'.**

AUNT AUGUSTA: Still, you could make as much noise with a stock whip as anyone—let's have a look at you then.

SYBYLLA *steps forward but her face remains largely hidden by her hat.*

Perhaps … without the hat.

SYBYLLA *begrudgingly removes it.*

I do hope—

SYBYLLA: [*revealing her face*] I don't. I don't look like my mother at all. I suspect you will find me a very ugly girl, Miss Beecham, and, in the absence of beauty, I wish I could confidently say that my moral character is without reproach or that I can play your piano with expected to above average ability, and though I am, I think, not quite all criminality, my hunger for music has not yet manifested in *actual* skill but I am glad to meet you and I'm very excited at the prospect of using your tennis court.

*Beat.*

AUNT AUGUSTA: Well. My nephew did say you were a different sort of girl—

HAROLD: Gussie, I only—!

AUNT AUGUSTA: Only said you were the best style of girl he'd ever met.

*Beat.*

Or did I get that wrong, Harold?

HAROLD: Don't mind my Aunt Gussie, Miss Melvyn; she's getting a bit doddery in her old age—

AUNT AUGUSTA: I'm forty-five, Harold—

HAROLD: And already losing your faculties—

AUNT AUGUSTA: I'm a woman in my prime—

HAROLD: And yet arrived there without learning to distinguish between matters that require your direct intervention and those that are none of your business. Senility, therefore, is the only conclusion I can come to.

*Beat.*

AUNT AUGUSTA: You know, Sybylla, there is no greater thrill than being told off by a young man you distinctly remember wetting himself—

HAROLD: Gussie—!

AUNT AUGUSTA: He demanded the right to relieve himself in that rose garden, and when I explained to him, for the umpteenth time, that the acidity was negatively playing with the soil composition, he squished his little face together and did his business in his trousers—

HAROLD: I was four years old!

AUNT AUGUSTA: You were seven— …

HAROLD: [*carting* SYBYLLA *off*] Alright. I'm sure Miss Melvyn doesn't want to hear any more stories—

SYBYLLA: Oh, but I do—!

AUNT AUGUSTA: [*yelling after her*] If you want stories, my dear, you know where to find me. I am a *trove*!

SYBYLLA: **But there is little time to sit and listen. The day is *hot*, and Mr Harold Beecham has two boats and a river to row—!**

HAROLD*, with mock naval insignia, and a terrible French accent:*

HAROLD: Aha! *Je te vois*, English scum! Down your sails at once—!

SYBYLLA: Avast, ye landlubber! Prepare to be scuttled!

HAROLD: You don't frighten me, you old sea dog! You may have beauty and brawn on your side, but I—I have sailed this tiny ocean a thousand times before—!

SYBYLLA: Tell me, swab! Be you Belgian or be you Dutch?

HAROLD: [*still French*] I am—I am *French*! I am a *French* admiral, leader of the *French* fleet—

SYBYLLA: Really! I had *no* idea!

HAROLD: [*still French*] And who are you: Lord Nelson or pirate—?

SYBYLLA: Arrgh, history has yet to tell—!

HAROLD: Then prepare your fleet, Pirate Nelson, as I ready myself to unleash the combined force of the Franco-Spanish Armada—

SYBYLLA *clambers from her own boat to* HAROLD*'s.*

—Nelson … you appear to be in my boat.

SYBYLLA: Don't worry yourself, Admiral Podge, I suspect neither of us will be in it for long …

SYBYLLA *straddles the edges of the boat and rocks it back and forth.*

HAROLD: Nelson …

Nelson, no.

Nelson— [*losing the accent*] —*Syb*.

Syb—you'll throw us both in—*Syb*—!

*They're flung out into the water.* SYBYLLA *disappears.*

Sybylla! Sybylla!

HAROLD *goes under to search for her. Comes up—nothing.*

*He goes under again. It's frantic, desperate.*

Syb …

Syb …

SYBYLLA *appears, soaked but unscathed, on the bank.*

SYBYLLA: Oh, for a picture of you.

HAROLD *wheels about.*

HAROLD: You could have—you could have *drowned*—!

SYBYLLA: Not I! I've been watching this last minute, Podgy, and it's abundantly clear I'm the stronger swimmer. No fear: I would have saved you had you gotten into any trouble— …

HAROLD: [*turning, averting his gaze*] Perhaps you should go inside.

SYBYLLA: [*accent back*] Arrgh, lost your nerve, Admiral—?

HAROLD: Before you— … before you catch your death of cold.

SYBYLLA *realises that the wet clothes cling to her body.*

*A moment.*

SYBYLLA: [*gathering her things, trying to laugh it off*] Death of cold? HA. Haven't you read any books, Harry? It's only good and pretty girls who are a blessing to everyone who die for such trifles; girls like I am always live to nearly ninety, to plague themselves and everybody else—!

## *EIGHTEEN: AUNT GUSSIE*

*Outside, on the lawn.*

AUNT AUGUSTA *is engaged in a farm task, hammering a post (or some such).*

AUNT AUGUSTA: So! Lady Melvyn! You thought high noon was the best time of day to take a bath?

SYBYLLA: My hair was dirty. It needed a good wash, I'm afraid.

AUNT AUGUSTA: It's a terrible waste of water, Sybylla, and in this drought—

SYBYLLA: I'm sorry, Gussie—

AUNT AUGUSTA: Are you?

*Beat.*

SYBYLLA: No. Not really.

AUNT AUGUSTA: Never apologise if you don't mean it, Sybylla—deflect, twist, manipulate—

SYBYLLA: 'How sorry I am you feel that way—'

AUNT AUGUSTA: That's better.

*She pats the ground next to her.*

Come. Dry yourself out here next to me.

SYBYLLA *flops onto the ground.* AUNT AUGUSTA *studies her.*

How is that mother of yours?

SYBYLLA: I don't know.

AUNT AUGUSTA: You don't write to her?

SYBYLLA: She doesn't write to me.

AUNT AUGUSTA: Nor I. When I was your age, your mother was my closest friend, and yet I haven't seen or heard from her since you all moved away. It seems strange to think of her as a mother of seven— …

SYBYLLA: Eight.

AUNT AUGUSTA: Eight, is it?

SYBYLLA: Ten, if you include the two that were lost.

*Pause.* AUNT AUGUSTA *absorbs this information.*

AUNT AUGUSTA: You know … I see a lot of dear Lucy in you.

SYBYLLA: There's nothing of dear Lucy in me.

AUNT AUGUSTA: Isn't there?

SYBYLLA: I'm like my father, everyone says so.

AUNT AUGUSTA: No child is a perfect copy.

SYBYLLA: My mother believes herself to be a saint.

AUNT AUGUSTA: Your mother is the only person I've seen to stand up to your grandmother. Marched right in there and said: Mother, *this* is the man I'm going to marry.

SYBYLLA: *My* mother—?

AUNT AUGUSTA: *Your* mother. Mrs Bossier gave Lucy all of five minutes to collect her things, and you know what Lucy did with those five minutes …?

She tried to take the piano.

She pushed that big hulking thing right through the house, only it damaged the floorboards so badly, your grannie was now more upset with a couple of scratches than she ever was with the impending marriage, so … I suspect that may have been your mother's plan all along.

*Pause.*

What do you think of my handsome nephew?

SYBYLLA: He's alright … I suppose.

AUNT AUGUSTA: Just alright?

SYBYLLA: I've heard he has a *terrible* reputation.

AUNT AUGUSTA: Does he?

SYBYLLA: Is that shocking that I just told you that?

AUNT AUGUSTA: It would be, if I weren't aware of it myself—

SYBYLLA: So he has a lot of women after him then—?

AUNT AUGUSTA: He certainly has a great many to choose from.

SYBYLLA: All after his property no doubt.

AUNT AUGUSTA: And you, Sybylla? What are you 'after'?

SYBYLLA: Oh … I wouldn't know how to put it into words—

AUNT AUGUSTA: [*putting down her work*] Why don't you try?

*She thinks.*

SYBYLLA: I want action …

I want *adventure* …

I want LIFE while young enough to live it—!

AUNT AUGUSTA: That's a lot to expect from a marriage.

SYBYLLA: Oh, I don't mean to ever marry—

AUNT AUGUSTA: Sorry—?

SYBYLLA: Marriage to even the best man in the world is a lowering thing—

AUNT AUGUSTA: Then why are you here?

*Beat.*

SYBYLLA: You— … you invited me—?

AUNT AUGUSTA: I didn't think you'd play my nephew for sport—

SYBYLLA: I can assure you, Gussie. Your nephew has not declared a single word of romantic affection towards me.

*Beat.*

AUNT AUGUSTA: And that … upsets you—?

SYBYLLA: No! Harry considers me a friend. Harry considers me a friend in defiance of convention that will have *no* friendship between a man and woman at all—! Why must *everything* be about marriage?!

AUNT AUGUSTA: I don't know. I suppose it's just the way it's always been.

SYBYLLA: You're not married?

AUNT AUGUSTA: My brother died. Leaving an estate to run and a child to raise—

SYBYLLA: And do you consider that luck or misfortune?

AUNT AUGUSTA: It is what it is—

SYBYLLA: Gussie.

*Beat.*

AUNT AUGUSTA: For eighteen years, I ran the estate myself. I was so busy with broken fences, the price of wool—a baby!—I barely had time to consider anything else.

And then … the baby grows up.

And he takes over.

And what are you left with except … yourself.

SYBYLLA: That doesn't sound so bad.

AUNT AUGUSTA: It's not. But it is lonely.

*Pause.*

Sybylla. Do you care for him—?

HAROLD *enters.*

HAROLD: Hello there, Gussie.

Sorry about the hair. It needed a good wash, I'm afraid.

HAROLD *sits down next to them.* AUNT AUGUSTA *looks between them.*

AUNT AUGUSTA: Hm.

HAROLD: Did you say something, Gussie?

AUNT AUGUSTA: Me? No. No, I was just … minding my own business.

*She exits.*

HAROLD *and* SYBYLLA *sit in silence, painfully aware of each other.*

HAROLD: I leave for Melbourne tomorrow.

SYBYLLA: Oh? How long?

HAROLD: Two weeks.

SYBYLLA: Two weeks is a long time.

*Pause.*

HAROLD: May I come visit you when I return?

SYBYLLA *smiles a bit.*

SYBYLLA: I can see no impediment to that, Mr Beecham.

HAROLD *smiles a bit.*

HAROLD: If you call me Mr Beecham again we may have to go for another swim.

SYBYLLA: Well, Mr Beecham, you could certainly do with the practice!

*He makes a run for her but* SYBYLLA *is flung back to Caddagat.*

**LIFE takes on a narrowness of focus.**

**When I make a pie, I think to myself, would he prefer apple or apricot filling?**

**When I play the piano, I wonder, is he a greater fan of Bach, Brahms or Beethoven?!**

**And through it all, I find myself *desperate* to know, is this the kind of man who prefers the company of animals or people—oh, what does it *matter*?!**

**There are a *million* things I want to do with my life, *none* involving—!**

AUNT HELEN: There's a ball at Five Bob this Saturday, if you'd like to go?

*Beat.*

SYBYLLA: … Is Harry back?

AUNT HELEN: Yes. Some time I think.

SYBYLLA: How long?

AUNT HELEN: Oh … two weeks, at least.

SYBYLLA, *in chaos.*

Jay Jay saw him in town last Friday, looking as sunstruck and handsome as ever, I'm told—!

SYBYLLA: **Two weeks and no visit.**

AUNT HELEN: [*fussing with* SYBYLLA*'s dress, oblivious*] A little tighter around the waist, I think—one or two inches should be enough—

SYBYLLA: **Two weeks and no visit.**

AUNT HELEN: I've ordered some new lace from Sydney—Oh, and do remember to wear a hat, Sybylla! You now have more freckles than you arrived with!

*The ballroom begins to form around them.*

SYBYLLA: **Two weeks and no visit!**

**What could possibly have occupied his time—?!**

## *NINTEEN: THE BALL*

MISS BLANCHE DERRICK *appears, all ruffles and plumes.* HAROLD *introduces* BLANCHE *to his guests.*

HAROLD: Miss Blanche Derrick.

BLANCHE: How do you do?

HAROLD: Miss Blanche Derrick.

BLANCHE: How do you do?

HAROLD: Miss Blanche Derrick.

BLANCHE: How do you do?

HAROLD Miss Blanche Derrick.

BLANCHE: How do you—?

SYBYLLA: Very well thank you. Gosh, it's hot, isn't it? Only I suppose you wouldn't be used to weather like this being from Melbourne and all?

BLANCHE: I suppose it is a bit warm?

SYBYLLA: Warm? It's the hottest day we've had all year—!

BLANCHE *laughs, a little too much.*

Are you—staying in town, or—?

HAROLD: Miss Derrick is our guest this weekend.

SYBYLLA: Really! That's … that's convenient—

BLANCHE: Convenient—?
SYBYLLA: No walk home for you—!
BLANCHE: Oh—!

*BLANCHE laughs and now much more than she should.*

SYBYLLA: If you'll excuse me, I think I— …

*SYBYLLA makes a beeline for the piano.*

FRANK: Ah, Miss Melvyn—!
SYBYLLA: NOT NOW, FRANK!

*SYBYLLA takes up the piano, pounding the keys in time, but with extraordinary force. BLANCHE's congenial laughter trails over the top, forming a bizarre sort of accompaniment.*

**This is not jealousy.**

**I am not the kind to be ruffled by such trivial emotions.**

**You must understand: of late, Mister Harold Beecham had attended on me so absolutely, I had unconsciously grown to look upon him as mine exclusively; and now, seeing him so suddenly monopolised, all prospect of fun is put to *wreck* and—**

HAROLD: Hello, Nelson.

*Beat.*

SYBYLLA: Podgy.
HAROLD: What are you doing there?
SYBYLLA: I'm playing the piano.
HAROLD: You seem to be destroying it.
SYBYLLA: It's the polka. It's supposed to be played with boundless enthusiasm.
HAROLD: Well. This is rather awkward, you see, because my dear Aunt Gussie, who is, in fact, the host of tonight's event, has requested, with comparable enthusiasm, that you kindly uh … stop.

*AUNT AUGUSTA glares at her. SYBYLLA stops, moves from the piano.*

Syb—wait—!

SYBYLLA: Mr Hawden, would you like to dance with me?
FRANK: Excuse me—?
SYBYLLA: Would you like to dance with me—?

FRANK: Dear girl—

SYBYLLA: Yes or no, Mr Hawden—

FRANK Surely it is I who must offer to—?

SYBYLLA: Frank. If you make me ask again, I fear the opportunity may pass.

FRANK *takes her hand.*

*They begin dancing.*

HAROLD *watches.*

FRANK *enjoys the closeness.*

FRANK: I must say, Miss Melvyn … you look *wonderful* tonight.

SYBYLLA: Do I, Mr Hawden?

FRANK: Your beauty, your uh, this uh, / this—

SYBYLLA: This dress?

FRANK: Yes! This dress! Like a hardy shrub in a desert storm—!

SYBYLLA: [*loudly, for* HAROLD*'s benefit*] Such poetry, Mr Hawden!

HAROLD *attempts to cut in.*

HAROLD: Excuse me—

Excu—

Mr Hawden, may I—?

*He forces himself between them and* SYBYLLA *immediately disentangles herself.* HAROLD *grabs at her, but she slips out of his grasp and escapes to the next room. The struggle is slight but not unnoticed by the guests.*

## *TWENTY: THE QUESTION*

*Alone and in the next room:*

HAROLD: Syb—wait—*wait*—!

*He grabs at her again, picks her up, she kicks at him. They tussle like children, ending up on the floor.*

Stop—I need to—what are you—? [*etc*]

SYBYLLA: [*overlapping*] Unhand me! Get your—*remove* yourself—! [*etc*]

HAROLD: Stop—Syb—please—I need to—I NEED TO ASK YOU SOMETHING.

*Beat.*

SYBYLLA: What?

What is it then?

What do you want to say to me—?

HAROLD: Would you just— … give me a minute to …

*He stands. Tries to get his breath back. Bolsters his nerve.*

Right.

Right.

It's no use making a long yarn about nothing. I'm sure you know what I want to say better than I do myself.

So.

Will it be a yes or a no?

*Beat.*

SYBYLLA: What is the question—?

HAROLD: What is—?

SYBYLLA: The question, yes.

HAROLD: Surely …? Surely you've known what I've been driving at ever since I first clapped eyes on you—?

SYBYLLA: I know you just carried me out of a room and dropped me on the floor—

HAROLD: Because you were being a foolish little minx—!

SYBYLLA: [*gasping*] *You—!*

HAROLD: —receiving the attentions of other men when—

SYBYLLA: I reserve the right to behave how I like without needing *your* permission—

HAROLD: —I could have any number of women—any number—!

SYBYLLA: Oh, Mr Beecham, you must not run away with the idea it is *yourself* they are angling for—!

HAROLD: How *dare* you speak to me like that—

SYBYLLA: [*as* BLANCHE] 'How do you do, how do you do—!'

HAROLD: She is a family *friend*—!

SYBYLLA: She's friendly alright—

HAROLD: [*leaving*] Oh, I know you like to appear cold and heartless, Sybylla, but I imagined there was *some* good underneath—it appears I was mistaken—

SYBYLLA: You've been back for *three* weeks!

*Beat.*

HAROLD: Yes, I— … I know—

SYBYLLA: You promised you'd see me—

HAROLD: I needed time to think—

SYBYLLA: About what—?

HAROLD: Marriage!

*Beat.*

Marriage, Syb.

SYBYLLA: To … to whom?

*Beat.*

No … *no*—

HAROLD: Syb—

SYBYLLA: I don't want to hear it—

HAROLD: I love you.

*Beat.*

I … I love you—

SYBYLLA: You don't love me—

HAROLD: Don't tell me what I— …! Do you have any idea what you've put me through?

SYBYLLA: We're friends, Harry—

HAROLD: Friends—!

SYBYLLA: We're very good friends—

HAROLD: Friends—

SYBYLLA: Dear old friends—

HAROLD: Do friends do this—?

*He clambers the space between them, grabs her and kisses her, forcefully, on the mouth.* SYBYLLA *struggles, reaches for something—anything—and—finding his whip—brings it down, hard, across his face.* HAROLD *exclaims and moves back. His forehead is split and bleeding.*

*He moves towards her, she thinks as if to hit her, but he grabs the whip from her instead.*

[*Bitterly*] A less stinging rebuke would have served your purpose, Miss Melvyn—

SYBYLLA: That was my first kiss.

*Beat.*

That was my first ever kiss and you *took* it from me.

*Silence.*

HAROLD *has no idea what to do. He takes out a handkerchief and removes the blood, embarrassed, ego bruised, but refusing to show it.*

*After a few moments:*

HAROLD: I'm sorry.

I'm sorry, Syb.

I should have— … I should have given some indication. I should have asked—

SYBYLLA: So ask.

*Beat.* HAROLD *puts the handkerchief away, moves towards her, stands as close as he can without touching her.*

HAROLD: May I?

SYBYLLA *nods.*

*They kiss each other. This time, cautious, unsure.*

*They part.*

*Silence.*

SYBYLLA: I don't know anything about you—

HAROLD: You do—

SYBYLLA: I've never heard you hold forth on a subject or a cause—

HAROLD: I'm not sure if you're aware of this, Syb, but it's sometimes hard to get a word in—

SYBYLLA: But you're always so calm, so unfailing good-tempered—?

HAROLD: And now you've seen my temper I suppose I've scared you off—

SYBYLLA: Oh no, I liked it so much I want to do it all over again.

*Beat. He grins.*

HAROLD: Me too.

*Silence.*

SYBYLLA: Apple or apricot?
HAROLD: … sorry?
SYBYLLA: Apple or apricot?
HAROLD: Apricot.
SYBYLLA: Bach, Brahms, or Beethoven—
HAROLD: Don't care. All dead.
SYBYLLA: Animals or people?
HAROLD: Animals.
SYBYLLA: Favourite animal—?
HAROLD: Pigs—
SYBYLLA: Pigs—?
HAROLD: You can't ask for more engaging companions—
SYBYLLA: *Pigs—?*
HAROLD: See! *See* how you cheered at the mere mention of pigs—!
SYBYLLA: I did! I—I *do*!
HAROLD: If you could have anything— …?
SYBYLLA: Anything—?
HAROLD: No restriction, no caveat—
SYBYLLA: Immortality.

*Beat.*

You're laughing at me—
HAROLD: I'm not—
SYBYLLA: If we could do away with death, we'd have infinite time to discover our strengths—think—*think* of what we could achieve—!
HAROLD: And what do you want to achieve?

*Beat.*

SYBYLLA: I don't know yet.

*Pause.*

If you could have anything …?
HAROLD: Without restriction—?

SYBYLLA: No restriction, no caveat.

*He considers this.*

HAROLD: My parents.

I'm not sure they needed 'infinite time', but … a few more years … I'd remember them, at least?

*An easy silence.*

*Then* HAROLD *takes out a small box.*

*They both stare at it.*

If I ask you to marry me—

AUNT AUGUSTA: [*off*] Harry? Harry?

HAROLD: What's your answer, Syb—?

SYBYLLA: I—I don't know—

HAROLD: You don't know—?

SYBYLLA: You had time to think—

AUNT AUGUSTA: [*off*] Harry—?

SYBYLLA: So I need time as well—!

HAROLD: [*pushing it at her*] You'll take the ring at least—?

SYBYLLA: I can't—

HAROLD: *Please*—

SYBYLLA: *No*—

AUNT AUGUSTA: [*entering*] Harry—?

HAROLD *and* SYBYLLA *part.*

HAROLD: Hi. Gussie.

*Beat.*

Miss Melvyn just—

AUNT AUGUSTA: Yes?

HAROLD: … Miss Melvyn just needed some air.

*Beat.*

AUNT AUGUSTA: And has Miss Melvyn had time enough to find it?

HAROLD: Perhaps. SYBYLLA: No.

HAROLD: No. SYBYLLA: Definitely not.

*Silence.*

AUNT AUGUSTA: Your aunt and uncle are looking to head home,

Sybylla. I will suggest to them that we keep you for the night. I'll get one of the servants to make up the back room and I expect you to be in that room before the sun comes up. In the meantime, perhaps the two of you might find that air … outside …?

… Where air is … bound to be …?

*She exits.*

SYBYLLA *studies the ring.*

HAROLD *watches* SYBYLLA.

*In the ballroom next door, music strikes up again. Perhaps the last of the guests gather around the piano to sing. Perhaps they use instruments. Perhaps it's nothing like this at all …*

HAROLD: Don't worry yourself, Syb.

You give me an answer when you're ready.

HAROLD *offers his hand.*

Come. I want to dance with you.

*They move out into the garden.*

*They dance together, gently, unceremoniously.*

*Around them, the colours begin to change.*

SYBYLLA: **When I began this story …**

**… I promised you it would contain nothing of sunsets …**

**… and I have kept my promise … because this …**

**…** ***this*** **…**

**… this is a sun*rise*!**

**I have seen them a thousand times before as I drag myself, heavy with sleep, out to greet another weary day, but on *this* particular day, the light glints through the leaves on the fern-banked stream and rises with the early morning mists and OH I am GONE …**

**I have lost my way …**

**I have fallen into trash descriptions of the most reprehensible kind!**

**The sky is a gentle orange pink. Tall trees surround us in striking silhouette. And the wind … the wind is *indeed* whispering!**

**But this is not a romance.**

**This is *not* a romance.**

**This is not a romance and yet … I have a ring on my finger …**

*And suddenly, she does.*

**I am wearing the stones on the palm side of my hand so that no-one will question it, and when I steal inside, close the bedroom door and undress …**

**… on my skin, I notice …**

**… many many marks.**

*She stands in her nightdress looking at herself in the mirror, equal parts thrilled and horrified.*

**I want to trace them all with ink so that when the bruises fade I will know *exactly* where his hands have been.**

**Here …**

**And here …**

**And here …**

**And here …**

**And here …**

*As* SYBYLLA *traces the faint bruises on her skin, her mother,* LUCY, *appears.*

LUCY: Dear Mother,

I suspect what I have to write will not be agreeable, so allow me to dispense with pleasantries and drive, instead, towards intent.

My husband has gotten himself into great debt and difficulties. He would have sold us all had it not been for the kindness of an old friend, who accepts, in lieu of repayment, the services of Sybylla as governess to his children.

No doubt Sybylla will have some opinion on the matter but remind her please to consider her little brothers and sisters.

Perhaps she will not find her new home as restful as Caddagat, but it is time she gave up pleasuring and began to meet the responsibilities of life.

Details enclosed.

Your loving daughter,

Lucy.

*A moment, then:*

SYBYLLA: NO—!

*Blackout.*

END OF ACT ONE

## ACT TWO

*ONE: BOAST NOT THYSELF OF TOMORROW*

SYBYLLA: No!

*No*!

No no no no no no no—!

GRANNIE: Your mother has already given her word—

SYBYLLA: I won't go! I can't! I *won't*—!

GRANNIE: Think of your little brothers and sisters—

SYBYLLA: Why should I?! Do you think Pa cared a jot for them before he drank up everything we owned—!

GRANNIE: You are the eldest, Sybylla. A child has a responsibility to their parents—

SYBYLLA: What about their responsibility to *me*? What about their responsibility to each and every child they alone decide to bring into this world?! I had no say in my existence! I've been given no say in any decision made about it since, and now *this*! No say in my indentured servitude—!

GRANNIE: Sybylla, *really*, there's no need for dramatics—

UNCLE JAY JAY: She has a point, Mother.

*Beat.*

… Lucy's approach does seem rather biblical in its zealotry …?

AUNT HELEN: To send a child to clear the father's debt?

UNCLE JAY JAY: It's not right—

AUNT HELEN: It's certainly unthinking—

UNCLE JAY JAY: But Lucy was always like that—even as a child—

AUNT HELEN: Hard-headed—

UNCLE JAY JAY: Hard-nosed—

AUNT HELEN: Perhaps you could write to her, Mother? Reason with her?

SYBYLLA: Oh, Grannie, please—!

UNCLE JAY JAY: What kind of money are we talking about here? Can't we just offer to make up the—?

GRANNIE: [*firmly*] No. We cannot. And need I remind you, this pitiless crow you speak of is the only one of my children *not* currently living off of my good graces. Moreover, she's given me eight beautiful grandchildren, which is, I've come to accept, more than I can hope from the two of you.

UNCLE JAY JAY *and* AUNT HELEN *fall silent.*

GRANNIE *turns her attentions to* SYBYLLA.

My dear Sybylla … I would not be willing to part with you under any circumstances, but I cannot interfere between a mother and her daughter—

SYBYLLA: Grannie—

GRANNIE: Enough. You won't have to stay there long. Give it two to three years—

SYBYLLA: Two to three years—!

GRANNIE: Give it two to three years and then I can have you back again.

*Silence.*

UNCLE JAY JAY: Practically … what are we to do about September—?

GRANNIE: [*warning*] Julius.

*Beat.*

SYBYLLA: September? What's happening in September?

*The* BOSSIERS *look between them.* GRANNIE *motions to* AUNT HELEN *to explain.*

AUNT HELEN: Your uncle had arranged for you and I to take a little trip to Sydney—

SYBYLLA: Sydney!

UNCLE JAY JAY: Just a … just a little trip. It was supposed to be a surprise for your birthday, but I'm uh … I'm afraid that—

SYBYLLA *runs.*

GRANNIE: Sybylla!

*Sybylla!*

*TWO: A BARGAIN STRUCK*

SYBYLLA, *in a rage, climbs up a tree.*

SYBYLLA: **Mother.**

***Mother.***

**The steel of her letter! That thin vein of satisfaction running right through the middle of it! Why does she not express just a *little* regret at the thing she is imposing on me? Two to three years away from Caddagat! Away from comfort and refinement! Away from Grannie and Uncle Jay Jay and dear Aunt Helen and a greater leap still from Sydney—unless—!**

HAROLD: Thought I'd find you here.

*Beat.*

SYBYLLA: ... Harry.

HAROLD: Should I come up there or do you want to come down here?

SYBYLLA: Grannie'll have a fit if she sees you up a tree with me—

HAROLD: [*already climbing*] So up to you then—

SYBYLLA *meets him with a kiss.*

She might also have some opinions on this.

*She stops him again with her kisses. Pulls him up the rest of the way.*

[*Looking around*] Syb—*Syb*—careful—

SYBYLLA: Let her see. Let them all see. I don't care who knows—[*turning the ring and shouting out*] —I want to wear this ring and proudly—!

HAROLD: Syb—

SYBYLLA: Yes.

*Yes*.

I'll marry you, Harry Beecham. I'll be your wife.

HAROLD *watches her for a moment, then turns.*

I ... I thought that would be happy news.

*Beat.*

There's someone else, I presume—?

HAROLD: No—

HAROLD: Miss Derrick, most likely—

HAROLD: Miss Derrick?

SYBYLLA: She'll make you a wonderful wife, Harry, kind and sweet, very good at—at laughing—

HAROLD: —laughing—?

SYBYLLA: —yes—it's a remarkable skill, Harry, really—

HAROLD: Syb—

SYBYLLA: So let's not speak any more on this— [*extending her hand*] —we'll be friends, good friends, as it was and as it should be—

HAROLD: I have *nothing* to give you.

*Beat.*

I'm broke, Syb.

The drought has been sitting on us for years. The price of wool has fallen, I—I thought I could shore up the place with investments, but now even those have failed, and— …!

*He pauses, contains himself.*

My only hope is that anything remaining is sufficient enough to support my aunt—

SYBYLLA: And what about yourself?

*Pause.*

HAROLD: The new owner has offered me the management of Five Bob.

It's a good job.

It's a fine job, in fact.

But I— … I can't quite stomach the thought of managing a place I've owned since birth, so I— … I don't know! The truth of the matter is, I don't know what I'm going to do. Take anything that comes up, I suppose.

*Silence.*

And now … it seems … you can't bring yourself to say anything to me.

SYBYLLA: I'm … I'm sorry for you, Harry.

*Silence.*

HAROLD: Yes.

Well.

Plenty worse off than me.

I'll start in Perth, I think. I've never been. It'll be good to put a bit of distance between me and the old place, and I— …

*He pauses at the base of the tree.*

… I can only hope that you find someone who will make you as happy as I would have tried to.

*He turns to leave.*

SYBYLLA: So. You think I'm the sort to care for a person only if he has a little money?

*Beat.*

HAROLD: What are you— … what are you saying, Syb—?

SYBYLLA: All my life, I've been no help to anyone—but here—*finally*—purpose—!

HAROLD: I don't [understand] —?

SYBYLLA: [*clambering down the tree*] I know what it is to be poor, Harry, I know what awaits you—!

HAROLD: Syb— …

SYBYLLA: We'll do it *together.* We'll face it proudly and bravely *together*—

HAROLD: Do you— … do you mean this—?

SYBYLLA: You are young and healthy, Harry Beecham. You have good character, and friends with connections, and friends with friends with connections! You still have your strength of spirit—

HAROLD: Of course I do—

SYBYLLA: —and I have mine! So perhaps—perhaps while you work to re-establish yourself, I could assist you—!

HAROLD: *Assist* me— …?

SYBYLLA: I have any number of ambitions, Harry—any number! Might it not be possible for me to attain at least one of them? Uncle Jay Jay thinks I could be an actress—imagine! Me! On the *stage*! And being *paid* for my performances—!

HAROLD: There's no need for that—

SYBYLLA: Or a singer, Harry—I could sing—it's an unusual voice, but it's not without merit—!

HAROLD: *No.*

*Beat.*

No.

That's not your burden to carry, Syb, it's mine.

*He grasps her face.*

All I need to know—*all* you need to say—is that you'll have me—and with that thought in mind, I know—I *know* I can turn things around—

SYBYLLA: Harry—

HAROLD: Say it. Say it again. Say you'll be my wife.

*Pause.*

SYBYLLA: If … I am of use to you—?

HAROLD: Like nothing else.

*Pause.*

SYBYLLA: Then …

… how can I turn my back on you now?

*They rest their foreheads against each other.*

HAROLD: I just need some time.

SYBYLLA: Time?

HAROLD: Two to three years—

SYBYLLA: Harry … Harry, no—

*But things are already beginning to shift.*

HAROLD: Two to three years to turn things around—

SYBYLLA: Two to three years—?

HAROLD: I'll come for you, Syb. I promise. I will—

SYBYLLA: Two to three years …?

**Two to three years …**

**Two to three years in—**

*THREE: BARNEY'S GAP*

MRS MCSWAT *bangs a large pot.*

MRS MCSWAT: DINNNNNEEERRRRRR!

*Mayhem. Plates and cutlery are thrown; chickens, pigs, dogs and small children removed from the table; but somehow, in its own well-oiled way, dinner begins.*

*The actors play any of the* MCSWAT CHILDREN *as needed—changing seats, positions and personas as fast as they can—thus contributing to the pandemonium.*

MR MCSWAT: So. What do you think of your new pupils, Miss Melvyn?

SYBYLLA *eyes the filthy* CHILDREN, *who all watch her suspiciously while shovelling food into their mouths.*

SYBYLLA: I, uh—

MR MCSWAT: [*indicating* PETER] You won't be teaching our Peter, of course—

CHILD: Peter's grow'd up.

CHILD: He's a man now!

CHILD: Got a moustache!

CHILD: An' a lady—

CHILDREN: [*making kissing noises etc*] Ooo, Suzie!

PETER: Shut it! You all shut it now!

MRS MCSWAT: [*to* SYBYLLA] You must be wondering, lovey …

SYBYLLA: Wondering?

MRS MCSWAT: Why our Peter's so big an' the rest so small. You see, we lost four little ones between Peter an' Lizer.

SYBYLLA: I'm so sorry, Mrs McSwat.

MRS MCSWAT: Five / years of hopin'—!

ALL MCSWATS: … years of hopin'—

MR MCSWAT: We didn't think we'd have another—

MRS MCSWAT: And then we did—

MR MCSWAT: And then we couldn't stop—!

MRS MCSWAT: Little miracles, each an' every one of them—

MR MCSWAT: [*counting them off*] Peter, Lizer, Tommy, Sarah—

MRS MCSWAT: Peter, Lizer, Tommy, *Katie—*

MR MCSWAT: Peter, Lizer, Tommy, Katie, Sarah, Jimmy—

MRS MCSWAT: *Jimmy,* Sarah—

MR MCSWAT: Mary Jane, Rose Ann—

MRS MCSWAT: Rose *Jane,* Mary *Ann—*

MR MCSWAT: Maggie, Arthur—

MRS MCSWAT: [*raising the baby*] Pip!

SYBYLLA: So … so how many children is that in total—?

MR MCSWAT: Well well well, the eddicatin' begins! Listen up, McSwats, if we've got six young'ns on this side, and four on this side, plus the one in your ma's lap—

MRS MCSWAT: And the four in the ground—

MR MCSWAT: As / loved as if they were here today—

ALL CHILDREN: … loved as if they were here today—

MRS MCSWAT: Well said, Pa, well said—

MR MCSWAT: Then we have a grand total of …? Well? Anyone?

CHILD: Six—!

MR MCSWAT: No, Jimmy—

CHILD: Three—

MR MCSWAT: Good try, Maggie—

CHILDREN: Five / Two—

MR MCSWAT: No—

CHILDREN: Eight / Ten / Seven—

KATIE: FOUR HUNDRED AND TWENTY-EIGHT THOUSAND MILLION.

MR MCSWAT: That is a BIG number, Katie. It's not the *right* number, but I'm mighty impressed you had the confidence to say it.

*He tickles* KATIE *and she squirms, delighted.*

MRS MCSWAT: You can see why they need their numbers, Miss Melvyn. I won't be expecting them to read a whole book, but if they're going to be successful business people like their pa then they'll need to be able to count.

MR MCSWAT: Say, do you play the peanny?

MR MCSWAT *indicates the decrepit-looking piano.*

SYBYLLA: A little, but—

MR MCSWAT: We were hoping you'd be able to—

MRS MCSWAT: It's just been sitting there gatherin' dust—

SYBYLLA: **And bugs and mice and rot in the wood—**

MRS MCSWAT: Did you say something, lovey—?

SYBYLLA: Just that I only play a little.

MR MCSWAT: A little's more than this lot can do, so come on, girl, let's be having it.

SYBYLLA *runs her fingers over the keys with gentle reverence.*

SYBYLLA: **A piano. Thank God. I would have, at least, one small comfort.**

*She plays a simple chord. It's horrifically off-key.*

MR MCSWAT: Oooo, would you listen to that!

SYBYLLA *tries again only it's a different sort of strange.*

EVERYONE: Oooo.

SYBYLLA *stops.*

CHILD: Why'd she stop, Pa?

CHILD: Make her keep going!

SYBYLLA: I can't. The keys stick. I push them down; they don't come back up again.

MR MCSWAT: Well, get Rose Jane over there to help you! You push 'em down, she'll pull 'em up.

SYBYLLA: There's also the problem of the missing keys?

MR MCSWAT: Still got a lot left, don't you?

SYBYLLA: Well, yes, but—

MR MCSWAT: So play the ones you have. Go on, girl. Give it a good whack.

SYBYLLA *does.*

SYBYLLA: **This is not any tune previously known to man. I am not playing from memory, I am simply striking the keys at random, and the louder the sound, the more they seem to like it—!**

*FOUR: PRINCIPALLY LETTERS*

SYBYLLA: **Dear Grannie,**

**I write to petition you for my immediate release from the**

**virulent pit of total benightedness in which my mother has imprisoned me—**

LIZER: Right—you've seen her prancin' about the place with her big hair and those fancy dresses—we're not going to listen to the likes of that—!

CHILD: No way—!

CHILD: No how—!

LIZER: Where did we send the last one who tried to teach us wot is wot—?

CHILD: To the madhouse—!

ALL: To the madhouse!

SYBYLLA: **The children, *not* through poverty, but on account of laziness, are the dirtiest urchins you have ever seen—as is everything else in this hot-oven house—**

*The* CHILDREN *empty mud, butter, honey—anything really—into* SYBYLLA*'s travelling cases, taking special care to smear it across her clothes.*

**—dirt in the oven, dirt on the table, dirt in one's soul and—**

*She opens her cases—*

No … no no no no no NO!

*The* CHILDREN *scatter, giggling.* SYBYLLA *locks herself away.*

**Dear Uncle Jay Jay—**

LIZER: [*banging on the door*] What are you doing in there, Miss Melvyn?

CHILD: Come out, Miss Melvyn!

CHILD: Yeah, come out!

SYBYLLA: **How is life at Caddagat without me—?**

MRS MCSWAT: [*shouting*] Leave her alone, Lizer, she's probably sleeping!

CHILD: Get a stick, Lizer!

CHILD: Yeah, get a stick!

*The* CHILDREN *poke at the door with sticks, try to put their little arms and faces through the cracks in the slab walls.*

SYBYLLA: **Is dinner conversation stilted and contrived?**

CHILDREN: Miss Melvyn—? / Miss Melvyn—? [*etc*]

SYBYLLA: **Does the piano sit silent in the corner—?**

CHILDREN: I can see you, Miss Melvyn! / Come out, Miss Melvyn! [*etc*]

SYBYLLA**: Send for me, Uncle, and you shall *never* know loneliness again—**

CHILDREN: [*beating at the doors and walls*] MISS MELVYN MISS MELVYN MISS MELVYN MISS MELVYN—

MRS MCSWAT *bangs a pot. Dinner.*

SYBYLLA: Jimmy, you have a perfectly good fork, try not to use your hands.

JIMMY: Pa does.

MR MCSWAT: And I'm a richer man today than them as didn't do it.

MRS MCSWAT: Well said, Pa, well said.

SYBYLLA: Lizer, don't put a whole slice of bread in your mouth, you need to cut it up first—

LIZER: [*her mouth full*] Ma doesn't—

MRS MCSWAT: [*laughing with her own mouth full*] You'll have your work cut out with this lot, Miss Melyvn …

SYBYLLA: Maggie—no!

MR MCSWAT: What? What did she do?

SYBYLLA: She threw her food on the floor.

MR MCSWAT: If she doesn't, what are the pigs and chickens supposed to eat?

SYBYLLA: With respect, Mr McSwat, if we put up a fence, the pigs and chickens wouldn't get inside the house.

MR MCSWAT: But then how do we keep the floor clean? Eh?

*The* MCSWATS *all lift their plates. The food slides to the floor.*

SYBYLLA: **Dear Aunt Helen …**

TOMMY: It's raining! It's raining!

SYBYLLA: **I am in hell.**

TOMMY: Everyone! Come out here! It's raining!

SYBYLLA: **There is nothing here to read, no functioning piano on which to play, and no-one to befriend as the neighbours taboo the place on account of its filth—**Tommy, please don't play in the rain—you'll catch a cold!

TOMMY: No, I won't!

SYBYLLA: And why's that?

TOMMY: 'COZ I'M A MAGIC BOOOOOOYYYYYYYYY

*He slides through the muddy water. Seeing the fun, the others join in, dancing in the rain and pushing each other in the puddles.*

SYBYLLA: **The only thing to do between teaching and washing and mending and minding is to sit still, tormented by maddening regret—**

TOMMY: [*racing back in, distressed*] Miss Melvyn! Miss Melvyn! I'M COLD! I'm cold I'm cold I'm cold I'm cold—!

SYBYLLA: Tommy—

TOMMY *sneezes in her face.*

**Dear Aunt Helen …**

*All the* CHILDREN *have come down with the same spectacular cold.*

**If I don't die of disease wrought by inadequate sanitation or any one of the pestilential children in my midst, I will surely die of monotony, so I beg you, Aunt, convince Grannie to take me back or bury me here, the choice is yours.**

MR MCSWAT *teaches* KATIE *how to kill sheep.*

MR MCSWAT: Peter, you hold the back legs; Tommy, you're on the front—

SYBYLLA: **Dear Aunt Helen,**

**Six letters, and no reply—**

MR MCSWAT: Katie, you make sure that knife is nice and sharp on that there rock—

SYBYLLA: **Either my mother has written instructing you against it, or you are devoid of any natural humanity—how else could you turn your back on the overburdened heart of a child—?**

MR MCSWAT: Alright, Katie—you ready—?

KATIE: Nooo—

LIZER: Let me do it, Pa!

KATIE: Let Lizer do it—!

MR MCSWAT: You've done it plenty, Lizer—

SYBYLLA: **Perhaps your husband, Colonel Bell, was right to abscond himself of you—**

MR MCSWAT: Quickly, Katie, right there, cross the neck—

SYBYLLA: **—for you are a rocky fount indeed in which to place one's love—**

LIZER: Come on, Katie—!

CHILDREN: Come on, Katie—!

KATIE: Ahhhh—!

SYBYLLA: [*overlapping*] **I have lost all respect for you, Aunt Helen—**

MR MCSWAT: Oh, Jesus *Christ*, Katie, you have to kill it before you start to skin it—!

SYBYLLA: **You are a cruel, loathsome woman, and I have no desire to ever see you again—**

LIZER: Let me do it, Pa—!

MR MCSWAT: Quick, Lizer—you better show her how …

LIZER *dives in and kills the sheep.*

AUNT HELEN *appears.*

AUNT HELEN: Dear Sybylla,

Thank you for your letters. I'm sorry for the delay but we have Gertie with us now; Jay Jay and I are taking her to Sydney and preparations have been all-consuming.

What a different sort of girl your sister is.

Sunny. Gentle. Kind.

Try to do good where you are.

Helen.

*FIVE: ED-JU-KAY-SHUN*

SYBYLLA*'s nerves are shot.*

*She writes a few letters on the blackboard, but the sound grates on her. She takes a moment to lean against it.*

LIZER, *noticing her distress, begins shoving her pen into the inkwell: 'tap tap tap'.*

SYBYLLA: Lizer.

Lizer.

Lizer, please, don't jab your pen like that, it'll spoil it.

LIZER: So?

SYBYLLA: If you spoil it you won't be able to do any work.

LIZER: Suits me jus' fine. Never asked fer any eddicatin'—

SYBYLLA: Ed-ju-kay—*shun*, Lizer, is important.

LIZER: Why?

SYBYLLA: It helps you get ahead in this world.

LIZER: Pa's not ed-ju-kay—*shuned* and he's a rich man—

SYBYLLA: Well yes, but—

LIZER: Your pa is and he's a worthless drunk wot has to give money to mine—

SYBYLLA: Lizer—

LIZER: You've been edjukayshuned too and you're only poor Melvyn's daughter wot has to teach us—

SYBYLLA: Lizer, I am going to give you one more chance.

*A brief respite. Then* LIZER *whacks the pen nib repeatedly against the ink well.* SYBYLLA *lunges for her, drags* LIZER *to the front, procures a switch.*

LIZER: Stop it—stop! Get off me! You get off me right now—!

*In a rage,* SYBYLLA *takes the switch to* LIZER*'s backside.*

MA MA MA MA MA MA MA—!

*The other* CHILDREN *join the yelling.* MRS MCSWAT *enters.*

MRS MCSWAT: What are you doing?! Stop! Get your hands off her—

SYBYLLA: Your daughter needs to learn some respect—

MRS MCSWAT: [*grabbing the switch*] Not like that she doesn't. Look at her—look what you did to her—you'd have had her dead if I hadn't walked in—

SYBYLLA: I barely touched her—

MRS MCSWAT: And you won't again.

Need I remind you, Miss Melvyn, my husband makes enough money, we could have had anyone out here. Someone from the city. Someone with proper training. But your pa's an old friend so we're doing him a favour, and that's what this is, do you understand me?

*She turns back to* LIZER *and scoops her up.*

Oh, my sweet girl … shh … shh …

*From her mother's arms* LIZER *sneers at* SYBYLLA. SYBYLLA *opens her mouth in a tiny howl of rage that grows into an almighty roar that takes us through to ...*

*SIX: A CONVERSATION*

SYBYLLA, *distressed, walks out into the moonlit scrub. Perhaps she cries out, kicks at, or throws a few things.*

*She slumps, exhausted in the dirt.*

*Looks up.*

SYBYLLA: Hello again.

It's been a while.

It's only the absence of anyone else to talk to that would bring me here and I thought I'd start by asking you a number of questions, ones I don't desire waiting on death to find the answer to.

Why did you make me this way?

Why fill me with cruel ambition and then set me down in a time and place where I can do *nothing* about it?

Perhaps you think I'm egotistical.

Is that it?

Do you want me to compress myself inside the *tiny* box it has pleased you to place me?

Egotism in myself must be stemmed and denied, but you—*you*—you must be fed on everlasting praise—and for what? You so loved the world you gave your only begotten son, then allowed that son to be nailed to a cross, achieving *nothing* as far as history shows!

Heaven knows what you would have permitted done to a *daughter*—!

PETER MCSWAT JNR *enters.*

PETER: Jeeesus Christ—

SYBYLLA: Peter—

PETER: Had you for a ghost, I did!

SYBYLLA: I was just going for a walk.

PETER: At night?

SYBYLLA: Between the washing and the teaching and the mending, and the minding, when would you have me walk—?

PETER: [*leaving*] If you want to walk then walk, doesn't bother me—

SYBYLLA: Wait!

Stay a while. Please.

I haven't spoken to anyone above the age of fourteen in all of eight months. I haven't read a book. I've run out of paper to write with. I feel like if I don't use my words, they'll all just die up inside of me, if they haven't already, and I just … I would really like to have a conversation? With someone. Anyone.

*Beat.*

PETER: Alright.

*An awkward pause.*

SYBYLLA: How do you like Barney's Gap?

PETER: It's fine.

SYBYLLA: How do you like working for your pa?

PETER: That's fine too.

SYBYLLA: Peter, what is your greatest ambition?

PETER: To marry Suzie, I suppose.

SYBYLLA: Anything else?

PETER: I'd like to make a lot of money.

SYBYLLA: To what end?

PETER: To keep Suzie happy, I suppose.

SYBYLLA: Don't you ever want anything more—?

PETER: More?

SYBYLLA: I just don't understand how *anyone* could stay in the same dark hole—

PETER: [*offended*] Right—okay—

SYBYLLA: —while the whole world outside teems with adventure—!

PETER: My pa comes from the other side of the world.

*Beat.*

Growing up, he was one of ten, the only one, his pa and ma included, that made it through the famine.

So he came here. Worked hard. Minded his own business and

ignored men when they started hating him for minding that business better than anyone else.

And times are tough, sure, they've always been tough, but I've never once gone to bed hungry. I'll never see my little brothers and sisters, my ma, my pa, *starving* to death in front of me, and it's *this* place that's given me that—right here—and I'm grateful to it.

*He shifts uncomfortably.*

I know that must be pretty small thinking to a smart girl like you, but— …

SYBYLLA: No.

*Beat.*

I envy you, Peter McSwat.

PETER: Right—okay—

SYBYLLA: No, I do. The cut of you has landed in the very sphere for which it was intended. You are going to be very happy in life, Peter … I'm sure of it.

PETER *beams. Then digs around in his bag and pulls out a magazine.*

PETER: Here. I buy these for Suzie to read but I'm sure she won't mind parting with one of them. I can't stand them myself but Suzie seems to like them well enough.

SYBYLLA *is touched by this small act of kindness.*

SYBYLLA: Peter— …

MR MCSWAT: [*emerging from where he's been watching them*] Peter McSwat. You're supposed to be on your way to Suzie's, are you not?

PETER: Just heading there now, Pa.

MR MCSWAT: [*to* SYBYLLA] You get inside, love. Mrs McSwat might be wanting some help.

MR MCSWAT *stares at her as she goes, somewhat troubled.*

SYBYLLA *studies the magazine:*

SYBYLLA: **'A Young Ladies Journal'.**

**The kind that has the latest fashions from Europe, socialite gossip**

**from Sydney, and short stories with pure-as-snow maidens awaiting thrilling rescue and extremely vague seduction.**

**In short, it's trash …**

**… and I *devour* it.**

## *SEVEN: NELLIE MELBA*

*Late at night.*

SYBYLLA, *in bed, tries to read by dull lamplight.*

SYBYLLA: [*reading*] 'For her reappearance at Covent Garden, Madame Melba selected the opera *Rigoletto*. Throughout the evening, her acting and appearance elicited the warmest admiration, her singing noted for its resounding fortitude. Indeed, Nellie Melba's pluck is such, she may have averted serious accident. During the second act, the stage wings caught fire and a sheet of flame erupted—!'

*A creak.* LIZER *enters.*

What are you doing?

LIZER: Yer lamp's keeping me awake.

SYBYLLA: Not my concern—

LIZER: I can't sleep!

SYBYLLA: Go to bed, Lizer—

LIZER: Please. What happens to Nellie?

SYBYLLA: So. You've been spying on me, have you—?!

LIZER: I just want to hear the rest of the story—

SYBYLLA: Story—?

LIZER: Is Nellie in a lot of fairytales?

*Beat.*

SYBYLLA: Madame Melba is a real person, Lizer—

LIZER: Nooo, she ain't no such thing.

*Beat.*

SYBYLLA: Back to bed—

LIZER: If I sit on yer bed like this …? If I sit on the edge here an' I don't even look at yer—yer can pretend I'm not here—right? Yer can pretend I'm not here and then yer can finish Nellie's story—!

SYBYLLA: Lizer—please—

LIZER: Not here, am I?

*LIZER stares determinedly to the front. SYBYLLA picks up the magazine again and begins to read.*

SYBYLLA: 'Before a threatened panic had time to develop, Melba stepped out, onto the stage, and assuaged the crowd with a verse of "*Caro Nome*"—'

*There's a pause as they both realise they're being watched by another CHILD, who hovers in the doorway.*

Come in if you like?

*The CHILD shuffles into the room. Clambers into bed with them.*

[*Continuing to read*] 'The fire was put out, the opera continued, but it was Nellie Melba's cool resourcefulness that had saved the day—'

*And then there's another CHILD—*

Hello there. Do you—?

*But the CHILD has already climbed into bed.*

'By command of Queen Victoria, a gala performance was announced in honour of the Shah of Persia. The Queen made known her wish that Melba should sing "*Caro Nome*" before the royal party …'

*As SYBYLLA, reads, LIZER begins to say the occasional word, until LIZER is reading them all by herself.*

## *EIGHT: 'CARO NOME'*

*Several months have passed and the family sits around LIZER, enraptured.*

*LIZER has covered herself in an odd but extravagant opera costume, very obviously made from things discovered around the home.*

LIZER: [*reading*] '… following—this—Madame—Melba—will—travel to … America. She—has—accepted—the sum of—forty—thousand pounds—'

MR MCSWAT: Forty thousand pounds!

EVERYONE: Pa! Shh!

LIZER: '—to sing—for—three months—'

MR MCSWAT: Forty thousand! For three months!

PETER: That's more than you, Pa.

MRS MCSWAT: A lot more, actually!

MR MCSWAT: Stuff an' nonsense is what it is. Lies to sell papers, most like. This Melber woman probably doesn't even exist—!

LIZER: [*passing him the magazine*] She does, Pa. I've got pictures an' everything!

MR MCSWAT: Why … this woman's *naked*! Forty thousand pounds and she didn't buy enough fabric to cover herself—!

SYBYLLA: It's an evening dress, Mr McSwat.

MR MCSWAT: [*passing the magazine to* MRS MCSWAT] It's scandalous is what it is. Her arms are out an' everything!

MRS MCSWAT: Ooo, Miss Melvyn, I hope you've never worn anything like this—!

SYBYLLA: Never—**not exactly never—**

LIZER: She wore this to a concert, Pa! [*Indicating her own costume*] Pearls on a string, a diamond crown in her hair—she sang before the King of Persia—!

LIZER *races to the piano, and, with the help of some* MCSWAT CHILDREN *(who lift the keys when they become stuck) stumbles through a verse of* 'Caro Nome'.

[*Singing*] *Caro nome che il mio cor*
*festi primo palpitar*
*le delizie dell'amor*
*mi dêi sempre rammentar!*

*Silence.*

MR MCSWAT: Did my Lizer just play the peeany?

LIZER: I did, Pa.

MR MCSWAT: And what language was that you were singing in—?

LIZER: I-talian, Pa.

MR MCSWAT: I-talian.

LIZER: Miss Melvyn says it's the language of music.

MR MCSWAT: *I*—talian! *My* Lizer!

SYBYLLA: She's a good pupil, Mr McSwat, when she puts her mind to it—

MRS MCSWAT: I don't remember languages or singing being on the list of things to teach?

*Beat.*

SYBYLLA: She wanted to learn—

MRS MCSWAT: And how's that going to help 'bout the place—?

SYBYLLA: Lizer, your father recently bought two bulls, he sold one for one pound four shillings, the other for one pound two shillings, making a loss of twenty per cent on the first, and a profit of forty per cent on the latter—did he make a profit on the whole transaction, or a loss? And how much?

LIZER: [*thinking a bit*] Profit. [*Thinking a bit more*] Four shillings.

*Beat.*

MR MCSWAT: Christ almighty, Lizer McSwat, I'll get you working at the sale yards tomorrow—!

MRS MCSWAT: Oh, no you won't—!

SYBYLLA: And there! There it is!

MRS MCSWAT: … What? What are you talking about—?

SYBYLLA: You bring me here to cultivate her mind, but only to the point she functions in the role you have determined—if I educate you anymore, Lizer, what am I cultivating in you but bitterness and rank disappointment!

*Silence.*

LIZER *starts to take the crown off her head.*

MRS MCSWAT: So. 'Sactly as I said, then. My husband—he didn't bring you here for none of that—

SYBYLLA: Lizer?

*Beat.*

Well *done.*

*Beat.*

MR MCSWAT: Yes … well done, Lizer—!

CHILDREN: Well done, Lizer! [*etc*]

MRS MCSWAT: [*a bit quieter*] Well done.

LIZER *smiles a bit, slides the crown back on.*

*Under the congratulations:*

PETER: Uhhh, Miss Melvyn?

*Beat.*

I'm uh … I'm not sure if you're aware of this? But tonight … tonight is an anniversary of sorts.

*Beat.*

SYBYLLA: Whose?

PETER: Yours—ours—all of us—I mean. One year ago today, Pa picked you up from that station, and … and you're a good teacher to the little ones, Miss Melvyn—

CHILD: Best we've had!

CHILD: Best we've had!

PETER: So uh … in thanks and uh thankfulness … we—together—all of us—I mean—decided to get you uh … this.

*A wrapped present.*

SYBYLLA: Oh. Peter. You shouldn't have …

PETER: Well, it's from all of us, so …

LIZER: Open it!

KATIE: Yer, open it!

SYBYLLA: Ooo, what could it be—!

KATIE: It's a notebook—!

PETER: Katie McSwat!

KATIE: What? It is, isn't it?

*And it is.* SYBYLLA *unwraps a notebook.*

PETER: You uh … you said you were worried about losing your words, or some such, so we uh … we thought to ourselves, well … we better get her something to write them all down in.

SYBYLLA *stares at the notebook.*

KATIE: Are you crying, Miss Melvyn?

SYBYLLA *is too overcome to respond.*

KATIE *threads her arms around* SYBYLLA*'s waist, and then the rest of the children follow suit, until it's only* MR *and* MRS MCSWAT, *standing off to the side, looking perturbed.*

*MRS MCSWAT not so subtly indicates that MR MCSWAT should say something.*

MR MCSWAT: Uh … Miss Melvyn.

Miss Melvyn, can we see you outside a minute?

*The hug continues.*

Miss Melvyn—!

*NINE: A BUST UP*

*Outside.*

SYBYLLA: I want to apologise to you, Mrs McSwat.

*Beat.*

MRS MCSWAT: Oh?

SYBYLLA: You are my employer; I had no right to speak to you that way—

MRS MCSWAT: Oh, never mind that, lovey, I know you didn't mean it—

SYBYLLA: I meant every word I said. Only I want to apologise for the rude way in which I said it—

MRS MCSWAT: [*stopping her*] Miss Melvyn. There's uh … there's something else we need to be talking about.

*She nudges MR MCSWAT.*

MR MCSWAT: Now er … I want to tell you … I don't— … I don't hold with a girl going out at nights to meet young men—

SYBYLLA: Sorry—?

MRS MCSWAT: No no, you let him finish. Go on, Pa.

MR MCSWAT: I uh … I have no problem with a girl co-'ortin' if it's a decent young man, I'd just prefer that co-'ortin' happened inside me own home, not out in the shrubs past midnight—

SYBYLLA: But—

MRS MCSWAT: Go on, Pa.

MR MCSWAT: And I— … I want you to know, I like you, Miss Melvyn, I like you well enough in yourself, so I'm sorry you've got smitten on our Peter—

SYBYLLA: Peter—?!

MRS MCSWAT: We need you to be sensible, lovey. Our Peter's good as made it with Suzie Duffy, we can't have you spoilin' it—

SYBYLLA: Mrs McSwat—

MRS MCSWAT: Now now, you don't need to hide it. We understand. Our Peter's a strapping lad—hard worker too—

MR MCSWAT: Wandering about the place in those tight trousers—if I was a young girl, I'd be clean gone on him meself—!

SYBYLLA: Mr McSwat, I can assure you, I have no intentions towards your Peter.

MRS MCSWAT: Well, our Peter certainly has intentions towards you.

SYBYLLA: I've given him no cause—

MRS MCSWAT: 'Cept that's not entirely true, is it?

You see, Miss Melvyn, apparently … apparently you tried to have a *conversation* with him.

*Beat.*

SYBYLLA: Well … yes, but—

MRS MCSWAT: And that conversation was such that our Peter has now convinced himself he's marrying you—

SYBYLLA: Marrying— … marrying *me*—?

MR MCSWAT: I have a lot of children, Miss Melvyn, and when the place is divided among 'em, it won't be much—

MRS MCSWAT: But ol' Duffy—he's only got two children—Suzie being one of them, so when her old man dies—

MR MCSWAT: She'll have a good bit of property to her name—

MRS MCSWAT: But you, Miss Melvyn, you haven't any property, not a bit of it—

SYBYLLA: [*laughing to herself*] Marrying *me*?!

MR MCSWAT: And we have other views for our Peter, which is why I need to be sending you—

## *TEN: BACK TO POSSUM GULLY*

SYBYLLA *and* LUCY *stare at each other.*

LUCY: What did you do?

SYBYLLA: Hello, Mother. Nice to see you too.

LUCY: You were supposed to stay there for two years.

*Beat.*

At *least*—

SYBYLLA: Would you like me to explain, or—?

LUCY: The debt has been paid off in full.

*Beat.*

[*Indicating the letter in her hand*] Mr McSwat informs me that your father needn't worry over the money anymore. 'What's the good in being alive,' he says, 'if we can't help each other out sometimes.' So, what I want to know is: … What did you do?

*Pause.*

SYBYLLA: The eldest son, it seems, took a liking to me—

LUCY: *Sybylla*—

SYBYLLA: And nothing happened. As you can see, Mother: Mr Peter McSwat Senior would rather let a significant debt slide than have me, Sybylla Melvyn, property-fraught daughter of one Richard Melvyn, marry into their family.

*Beat.*

LUCY: Do you … have feelings for the boy?

SYBYLLA: Consternation, mainly—

LUCY: Then why—?

SYBYLLA: He was kind to me. So I was kind to him. And apparently, that, in his eyes, became a contract of sorts.

LUCY: It can do, yes, if you're not careful, and knowing you, I imagine you weren't—

SYBYLLA: I spent twelve months in that stinking hovel, Mother! I did it for you! For the children—!

LUCY: You only did it because I told you to—

SYBYLLA: A kind word.

*Beat.*

One. Just one.

*Pause.*

LUCY: Well. It seems it was possible for you to find a worse place than home—

SYBYLLA: [*already gathering her things*] No matter. I won't be here long.

LUCY: And where are you going to go—?

SYBYLLA: Back to Caddagat, of course—

LUCY: Caddagat—?

SYBYLLA: Grannie'll have me—Grannie'll be happy to have me—

LUCY: Grannie has Gertie now—

SYBYLLA: She's been up there a year—it's my turn now—

LUCY: Gertie is staying there—

SYBYLLA: Because she's sunny and gentle and kind—!

LUCY: Because she's soon to be engaged.

*Beat.*

SYBYLLA: She's a child.

LUCY: She's almost sixteen.

SYBYLLA: And what aspiring young gentleman has Grannie thrust upon her—?

LUCY: Mr Harold Beecham.

*Beat.*

SYBYLLA: … Harry?

LUCY: It's a shock, I know. Imagine. Our Gertie, mistress of Five Bob Downs …

SYBYLLA: He's supposed to be in Perth.

LUCY: Not anymore—

SYBYLLA: He lost all that money—

LUCY: Well, it's certainly found him again. Some old sweetheart of Harold's father died and left her wealth to him. Grannie says he's repurchased Five Bob and is now spending an almost indecent amount of time with Gertie. Apparently, we should expect him soon on a little 'asking expedition'—

SYBYLLA *turns.*

Now, Sybylla … we must be happy for Gertie.

I know … I know it's not ideal to have a younger sister married before the first—

SYBYLLA: It's essentially my death knell and we both know it—

LUCY: Sybylla—

SYBYLLA: I'll never hear the end of it from you: darling Gertie, married, and problem Sybylla, forever at home, forever under your feet—that's what you fear, isn't it?!

*Beat.*

LUCY: Have I ever pushed you to marry—?

SYBYLLA: Not now, Mother—*please*—

LUCY: No—have I ever set you in that kitchen, serving tea, to a string of eligible young men—?

SYBYLLA: Perhaps you feared I wouldn't make a match—

LUCY: With ten men to every woman, Sybylla, you can have your pick—

SYBYLLA: Wonderful—let's begin—!

LUCY: Is that what you want?

*Beat.*

All I have ever done is try to help you take stock of your possibilities—

SYBYLLA: What possibilities—?!

LUCY: I want you to have your own income—

SYBYLLA: You sent me off to be a little bush-school teacher—

LUCY: And if you were worth an inch, you would have stayed there!

*Beat.*

You seem to live in a dream world, Sybylla, where the undeniable fact of your sex will be ignored—nay—celebrated!

But I live in this one.

And if my daughter cannot thrive in it, I want her to at least survive it.

*Pause.*

If you find yourself … now … wanting to marry, I promise … I will support you in that, but— …

I was trained in nothing but marriage.

And this, Sybylla …

*She looks around her 'lot'.*

… I wouldn't wish this on anyone.

LUCY *exits.*

SYBYLLA *remains with her thoughts.*

SYBYLLA: **Harry …**

**…**

**Gertie …**

**…**

**…**

**All this time …**

**All this time … I thought …**

**Instead … it appears—**

*ELEVEN: LITLE BROTHER*

HORACE: The McSwats kicked you out, did they?
SYBYLLA: Horace!
HORACE: Big sister.
SYBYLLA: I can hardly call you little brother anymore!
HORACE: Taller than Pa now.
SYBYLLA: I'm sure that comes in handy …
HORACE: I'm glad you're back.
SYBYLLA: Well … with Gertie gone, I assumed you'd need someone else to bait—
HORACE: I'm leaving, Syb.

*Beat.*

I tried to go last year. Ma said the little ones would starve if I did, but the boys are coming on like haystacks and you're back now, so … so …

*Beat.*

… you don't mind, do you?
SYBYLLA Horace. You can't leave—
HORACE: I'm not busting myself day and night so Pa can go off and swallow the proceeds—
SYBYLLA: So take over! The place'll be yours soon enough, why not get a head start—?

HORACE: It won't be mine—

SYBYLLA: Ours then! You and I! We could make a business yet! Let me *help* you—

HORACE: I'm going to America.

*Beat.*

Uncle Jay Jay got me a job up north. Pays well too. I'll work that for a year, then take a boat out of Cairns—

SYBYLLA: And what about me—?

HORACE: What about you?

*Beat.*

You've been two places now; I haven't been any—

SYBYLLA: Horace—

HORACE: I have been *stuck* here—two whole years—ploughing—milking—working so hard I can't *sleep* for the pain—while you—Gertie—go off having all kinds of adventures—!

SYBYLLA: And you're right to go.

*Beat.*

It was good of you to stay as long as you did. I'm grateful—

HORACE: Don't start—

SYBYLLA: I mean it. Thank you.

*A long silence.*

HORACE: Do you remember when Pa bought this place?

He said the finest thing about it was this road. Direct from the front paddock to the city of Goulburn …

SYBYLLA: … from there, a train to Sydney …

HORACE: … and then onto a sea track / that meets the world.

SYBYLLA: … that meets the world.

HORACE *climbs up onto the front gate (or some such).*

HORACE: I used to climb up here. See if I could catch a glimpse of it.

SYBYLLA: Me too.

HORACE: Took me months to realise we were a hundred miles away from anything resembling ocean.

*Beat.*

SYBYLLA: Me too.

*Silence.*

Write to Mother.

HORACE: I will—

SYBYLLA: I mean it, Horace.

Remember her. Please.

HORACE *climbs down and departs.*

SYBYLLA *opens her mouth as if to say something to the audience.*

*Finding no words, she closes it again.*

## *TWELVE: LIFE—CONTINUED*

RICHARD *staggers home drunk.*

SYBYLLA *leads the way.*

RICHARD: [*singing*] The troubles of life are many
The pleasures of life are …
When we sat in the … Annie,
I dreamt that the skies were …
When we sat in the …
I dreamt that the …

*He stops to urinate.*

SYBYLLA *waits.*

… Did you hear the news, Sybbie?

*No response from* SYBYLLA.

The last of the colonies has signed up. All it needs now is the Queen's approval, and you and I … we'll be living in the newest nation on earth before the year is out …

*No response from* SYBYLLA.

Aren't you excited, my girl? There's no longer any need to inherit sin or sorrow from abroad! Change … *real* change is about to happen—I'll make sure it does—

SYBYLLA: What do you mean by that?

*Beat.*

RICHARD: I'm going to run for parliament.

*Beat.*

I'm no businessman, Sybbie, but I might have some ability yet as a statesman—

SYBYLLA: How are you going to raise the funds?

RICHARD: Any number of ways! Any number! A little commonsense, a lot of passion—

SYBYLLA: Pa—

RICHARD: —and you! You could canvass for me! You might even have some of this same ability, so—so while you're helping your old man gain his seat, why don't you educate yourself in—in readiness for the time when you can too—!

SYBYLLA: Oh, Pa—stop!

*Beat.*

Please, just— …

SYBYLLA *continues on.*

RICHARD *trails behind her.*

## *THIRTEEN: LIFE—CONTINUED, CONTINUED*

*Some or all of the following occur.*

SYBYLLA *scrubs.*

SYBYLLA *milks.*

SYBYLLA *churns butter with her mother.*

*Little sister* GERTIE *appears in a beautiful new dress, enjoying the relative comfort of Caddagat.*

SYBYLLA *bakes.*

SYBYLLA *whitens the hearth.*

*A bushfire.* SYBYLLA *helps* RICHARD *and* LUCY *to put it out.*

GERTIE *races through the grounds of Caddagat,* HAROLD *in pursuit. He picks her up, tussles with her like a child. Perhaps he gives her a pirate hat. Perhaps he rows* GERTIE *down the river.*

SYBYLLA *shines pot lids.*

SYBYLLA *sweeps.*

SYBYLLA *collects the washing with her mother.*

HAROLD *dances with* GERTIE. *Perhaps* GRANNIE *watches on.*

LUCY *visits two small bush graves. From some distance,* SYBYLLA *watches her mother.* LUCY, *unaware of* SYBYLLA*'s presence, tidies the graves then stands in quiet observance.*

SYBYLLA *continues on to collect her father.*

SYBYLLA *scrubs.*

SYBYLLA *milks.*

*And through it all,* SYBYLLA*'s clothes might collect the dirt, soot, suds and grime of this 'sodden round of grinding tasks'.*

*She is, in her own words (if she had any) — 'inured to her yoke'.*

*Several months pass. ...*

## *FOURTEEN: A VISITOR*

*A tired and emaciated calf has fallen in the mud.*

SYBYLLA: Come on, little darling … get up … get up …

*She pulls.*

Get up!

*She pulls.*

Get up!

*She pulls.*

Please! Please get up—*please*—you *stupid* beautiful thing—if you stay down, you die—if you stay down, you die—and you will *not*—do you hear me?—you will *not—!*

HAROLD: Hello there.

*Beat.*

SYBYLLA *doesn't turn.*

Can I help at all?

*Beat.*

SYBYLLA: … Harry.

HAROLD: It would pay better to shoot the poor little beggar now—

SYBYLLA: Perhaps to someone with a princely herd, but here we have to be more careful—

*HAROLD rolls up his sleeves and dives in.*

No!—Harry—!

*But he's already in the mud, and, within seconds, has re-roped the calf with considerable skill.*

HAROLD: Alright, on the count of three—one—two—*three*—

*They pull and the calf is lifted.* HAROLD *releases the rope and* SYBYLLA *falls in the mud.*

Oh! Oh, Syb—!

SYBYLLA: [*laughing*] It's fine! [*Pointing at the calf*] She's up—she's up!

HAROLD: Here—let me—

SYBYLLA: Don't. I wouldn't want the new owner of Five Bob getting his clothes all dirty.

HAROLD: You heard, did you?

SYBYLLA: Grannie's letters are full to overflowing.

HAROLD: The old woman left me nearly a million—imagine—!

SYBYLLA: Imagine!

*Beat.*

HAROLD: Syb. I'm not ungrateful for my time without—

SYBYLLA: I'm sure—

HAROLD: It made me a better man—I needed to know—

SYBYLLA: How glad I am it proved such an edifying experience for you—

HAROLD: I didn't ask to be put in some stranger's will—

SYBYLLA: And yet. You are exactly the kind of person I would expect providence to favour.

*Beat.*

HAROLD: Why do I always suspect there are four or five different meanings in what you say— …?

SYBYLLA: [*moving back towards the house*] Oh, I hardly know what I mean most of the time—let me go find Pa for you—

HAROLD: I don't need to speak to him just this minute—

SYBYLLA: You don't need to worry, Harry. He'll be pleased.
HAROLD: I do hope so—
SYBYLLA: Gertie is going to make you the most wonderful wife—
HAROLD: Gertie—?
SYBYLLA: Be kind to her, Harry—be good, and honest, and warm—
HAROLD: It's not Gertie I want to marry, Syb … it's you.

SYBYLLA *stops.*

SYBYLLA: I— … I thought— …?
HAROLD: Gertie? You thought I wanted to marry Gertie—?
SYBYLLA: Why— … why wouldn't you—?
HAROLD: She's your sister.

*Beat.*

SYBYLLA: Yes, she is—
HAROLD: So mine too!

*Beat.*

I— … I would have written sooner. Only you remember our bargain, and I was just waiting to get things fixed up a little, and now they are—fixed, I mean, and— … [*approaching suddenly to kiss her*] … well, I can have you now—
SYBYLLA: Oh, Harry—wait!

*He stops short.*

HAROLD: What?

What is it?

You didn't mean your promise—?
SYBYLLA: Of course I did—
HAROLD: There's someone else—
SYBYLLA: No—
HAROLD: Frank Hawden, most likely—
SYBYLLA: No! *No*. No, it's just— …

*Beat.*

Harry!

You— … you want to marry me—?
HAROLD: Yes—!

SYBYLLA: Are you— … are you *sure*—?!

HAROLD: My God! Syb! Fifteen months! I've thought of almost nothing else—!

SYBYLLA: But I still don't— … you and I, we— … we barely know each other—

HAROLD: I like apricots, remember? I can't tell Bach from Beethoven. Pigs are the *greatest* animals—Syb, we can keep learning each other for the rest of our lives—

SYBYLLA: But I don't really know what it is you *offer,* Harry—

HAROLD: You can have what you like—

SYBYLLA: Do you want to have children—?

HAROLD: [*shocked*] Syb.

*Beat.*

SYBYLLA: Do you … want to have children …?

HAROLD: That's not— … that's not something—

SYBYLLA: You don't need to be coy with me, Harry Beecham. We're both farmers; I know how it works.

*Beat.*

HAROLD: When you … when you marry someone … children are, of course—

SYBYLLA: A consequence.

HAROLD: A consequence?

SYBYLLA: Yes.

HAROLD: I was thinking more … more a *delight*—?

SYBYLLA: If you have the time to enjoy them. If you get to dip in and out of their care while having a life—a life!—of your own. But I'll be the one who carries them. Me. Once a year, every year—until my body finally gives it up or I die, oh God, whichever comes first, and parties, Harry—*parties*—

HAROLD: Parties—? / I don't—?

SYBYLLA: —every luncheon, every dinner, every dance, every godforsaken event, I will stand there on your arm, and you will introduce me—my wife—!

HAROLD: Of *course*—

SYBYLLA: —my—my *wife*—

HAROLD: Yes—my wife—!

SYBYLLA: —and I know you find me interesting, Harry—I know—I know I puzzle and—and *amuse* you—but I also know you think—like everyone else—that life—*real* life—will *beat* that out of me—

HAROLD: *Syb—*

SYBYLLA: —and one day—one day you will ask me to attend some matter of your concern, and I will say—'I cannot, dear husband. I have my own matters to attend to'—and you will— … you will *laugh* at me, Harry—

HARRY: I won't—

SYBYLLA: —you will *laugh—*

HAROLD: Always telling me / what you think I—!

SYBYLLA: You will—of course you will—!

HAROLD: And in this grand list of things that haven't happened, I suppose you can't think of a single time I make you *happy*—?!

SYBYLLA: I can think of so many!

*Silence.*

HAROLD: Sleep on it, Syb.

I'll pitch a tent near the house.

We'll go for a walk in the morning—find some river or muddy dam—you can push me in, if you like—I don't care—!

SYBYLLA: No.

No … is my answer.

HAROLD *doesn't know what to do with this response. He's not used to being emotional in front of a woman—he's not used to being emotional—and he turns—tries—badly—to squash it.* SYBYLLA, *in turn, tries—badly—to explain herself.*

I … I've been so long now without the idea of you, that I— …

*Beat.*

I can't— … I can't give myself up, when— …

*Beat.*

In the years to come … in the years to come, it will always be a great comfort to me—

HAROLD: [*to himself*] Comfort?! [*Laughing bitterly*] Comfort …

SYBYLLA *watches him.*

*She approaches him slowly.*

*Reaches out a hand and rests it on his shoulder. He doesn't shake it off so she doesn't remove it. She moves closer, and closer, until her whole body rests against his back.*

*They stand like this for some time.*

*Eventually he turns and they rest their foreheads together. She whispers:*

SYBYLLA: May I?

*He laughs a little, surprised.*

*She holds his face in her hands and kisses him.*

*Perhaps she smudges a little bit of mud on his face for good measure.*

*Perhaps he follows suit.*

*Then* SYBYLLA *steps away.*

Safe journey home, Mr Beecham.

*Silence.*

*Then:*

HAROLD: Goodbye, Miss Melvyn.

HAROLD *walks away.*

SYBYLLA *watches him go.*

*Tussles with herself.*

*She runs after him.*

*Stops herself.*

*Moves again as if to go.*

*Stops.*

*Moves.*

*Stops.*

SYBYLLA: ...

...

**Every time …**

**…**

**…**

**Every time I try to breathe it down, it comes back fierce and loud, and it says …**

**More.**

**Give me *more.***

**…**

**…**

**…**

**Will it get a hearing?**

**…**

**I don't know.**

**…**

**But time is thorough in his work …**

*FIFTEEN: … SOMEHOW …*

*As* SYBYLLA *talks, her mud-soaked clothing is removed and replaced.*

SYBYLLA: **My father, days before harvest, decides to run for local parliament.**

**On a podium, he excels. In fact, almost wins. But the expenses are so heavy, we beg him not to run again.**

**Horace makes it to America.**

**No more is heard.**

**Gertie, at Grannie's pressing, accepts a proposal. From one Mr Frank Hawden. She has time to send three deliriously happy letters. After a difficult birth … the letters stop. Grannie writes instead …**

**… 'It was God's will,' she says.**

**Harold abstains from marriage longer than I thought he would. He hands management of Five Bob back to his aunt. He travels the world. He deems destiny responsible when he meets his**

**future wife, and he begins to mend his heart around his growing brood.**

**The cow … by some strange miracle … lives long enough to sell.**

**It sees us through to Christmas, and then Christmas, distinguished only by plum pudding and a few bottles of homemade beer, has been once again.**

**And somehow … it is 1899 … and we stand on the edge of a new century.**

**Still …**

**… here I am.**

**Sharing a bed with my siblings.**

**Listening to my parents bicker through the cracks in the walls.**

**…**

**In truth … there are a *million* things I want to do.**

**But I have taken stock of my possibilities …**

**… as they genuinely exist …**

**… and found one … where the implements of trade and wellspring of inspiration, are, already, in my possession.**

SYBYLLA *takes out a pen and the notebook gifted to her by the McSwats.*

**Dear Sirs,**
**This story is all about myself.**
**For this … I make no apologies.**

*In the late hours of the night,* SYBYLLA *writes.*

LUCY *enters.*

LUCY: The cows, Sybylla—

SYBYLLA: [*without looking up*] Locked away for the night.

LUCY: And the dinner things—?

SYBYLLA: Washed. So are the clothes.

LUCY: Where are the little ones—?

SYBYLLA: In bed—the older ones too, and Mother, I have one hour, one precious hour, that is mine and mine alone, and I ask that you please—*please*—allow me that hour in its entirety.

LUCY *fights the automatic urge to respond.*

*Doesn't.*

SYBYLLA *continues writing.*

LUCY *moves to the stack of dishes. The folded clothes. The chores are, indeed, all completed.*

*Needing to keep her hands busy,* LUCY *sits and moves to do some mending, then puts it down, unsatisfied.*

*The piano is in her periphery. She's drawn to it but also scared of it. After a few moments, she moves to the old upright, opens the lid, and touches the keys.*

*She plays a few gentle bars and then feels* SYBYLLA *staring at her so stops.*

LUCY: If I'm disturbing you …

SYBYLLA: No. Not at all.

LUCY: I should find something else to—

SYBYLLA: Please. Don't stop. [*Indicating her own writing*] It helps … I think?

LUCY, *still unsure, settles back at the piano.*

*She plays, slowly at first, out of practice, but growing in confidence. The sound under* LUCY*'s hands is beautlful, for many reasons, not least of which because this old piano is finally being used by its owner for the purity of her own enjoyment.*

SYBYLLA *returns to the page allowing her mother's music to galvanise her as she writes.*

LUCY *plays.*

SYBYLLA *writes.*

*And a tiny oasis is formed.*

*The lights slowly fade to black.*

END OF PLAY

## STELLA MILES FRANKLIN TIMELINE

**1788** Franklin's ancestors arrive on the First Fleet.

**1810–1840** White settlers seize the lands of the Wiradjuri, Ngarigo, Ngunawal, Jatmatang and other peoples of southern NSW.

**1879** Stella Miles Franklin born at Talbingo, near Tumut, to a family connected with squatting interests.

**1887–1892** Gains a rudimentary education at local schools.

**1890–1901** A severe economic depression hits Australia and drives families from their farms.

**1890s** Franklin works on the family's diminishing landholdings, does some nursing, starts her journal.

**1897** Franklin works as a governess at a squatter's station near Yass.

**1898** Begins writing *My Brilliant Career* from her family's small dairy farm outside Goulburn.

**1900** Submits the manuscript to Henry Lawson, who shows it to his publishers in Scotland when local publishers are lukewarm.

**1901** Australian colonies federate to become a sovereign country

**1901** *My Brilliant Career* is published by Blackwood. It becomes an instant success and the first local bestseller of the new nation.

**1902–1905** Franklin tries to establish herself as a writer in Australia, turns down several marriage proposals. Works as a servant in Sydney. Writes about her experiences but is unable to find a publisher.

**1906** Moves to the USA, where she works for the National Women's Trade Union League and is editor of the journal *Life & Labor*.

**1915** Australian forces fight at Çanakkale (Gallipoli).

**1916–1917** Franklin works at childcare centre in Deptford, London, and at nights as a cook at a cafe in High Holborn.

**1917–1918** Volunteers with a hospital attached to the Serbian army as cook and orderly.

**1919–1926** Works as a secretary for the National Housing and Town Planning Association in London.

**1906–1927** During this period, Franklin completes several new novels and plays but struggles to find a publisher or a producer.

**1927** Returns to Australia, and the family home in Grey Street, Carlton, Sydney.

**1928–1931** Publishes successful pastoral novels under the pseudonym 'Brent of Bin-Bin'.

**1930s** Forms friendships with a number of right-wing nationalist writers, and expresses ultranationalist positions.

**1931** Franklin's father John Franklin dies, aged 84.

**1936** *All That Swagger* published.

**1938** Franklin's mother Susannah Margaret Franklin dies, aged 88.

**1940s** Actively champions Australian literature and writers. Becomes a constant attendee at cultural and literary events.

**1941–1945** Despite her misgivings about war, Franklin works for the welfare of the troops and raises money to support the Soviet forces.

**1946** *My Career Goes Bung*, a sequel to *My Brilliant Career*, published.

**1954** Franklin dies on 19 September, aged 74. Her ashes are scattered at Jounama Creek, Talbingo, close to where she was born.

**1957** In her will, Franklin makes a bequest to establish an annual literary award: The Miles Franklin Award. The first winner was Patrick White with *Voss*.

**1963** Franklin's memoirs, *Childhood at Brindabella*, published posthumously.

▼ ▼ ▼ ▼ ▼ ▼ ▼